Judith Ellen Foster

The Crime against Ireland

Judith Ellen Foster
The Crime against Ireland
ISBN/EAN: 9783743418691
Manufactured in Europe, USA, Canada, Australia, Japa
Cover: Foto ©ninafisch / pixelio.de

Manufactured and distributed by brebook publishing software (www.brebook.com)

Judith Ellen Foster

The Crime against Ireland

THE CRIME AGAINST IRELAND

BY

J ELLEN FOSTER

WITH A PREFACE BY

JOHN BOYLE O'REILLY

BOSTON
D LOTHROP COMPANY
FRANKLIN AND HAWLEY STREETS

PREFACE.

THIS book, I take it, is one of the latest illustrations of the Irish power of conversion or assimilation. Mrs. Foster went to Ireland with no bias in favor of the people or their national cause ; and she came away not only a convert, but a missionary, and one of the most eloquent and impressive of those who tell abroad the tale of afflicted Erin.

Were it not for this converting power there would be no worldly hope for the weak who were oppressed. The earth would belong to the strong and the ravenous. For instance, the chains that were bound on Ireland by Cromwell in 1642 would still hold on the chafed limbs. Cromwell gave the land of Ireland to English soldiers — every acre of it except the province of Connaught. But where is the Cromwellian now in Ireland? He has disappeared like a stone thrown into a lake, or rather like a fierce storm of hail driving violently into the breast of a lake, and melting at once into its kindly flood.

This same power is going on outside Ireland; and Mrs. Foster's book is one of its restless reachers and tentacles. In a certain way, England and Ireland represent essentially different human forces : one the force of impact, of organization, of pressure, of individualized greed — in a word, of *concentration*. The other, the very opposite — as steam is to water — the

Preface.

power of diffusion, expansion, neglecting organization to win opinion, preferring to make all men of one mind to making a few men of one body.

By this means, Ireland, having failed to shake off the English grip with a weapon, is succeeding with a word. Instead of a hopeless, but heroic pike against a long-range rifle, Ireland has learned to depend on a weapon that carries farther than a cannon — patient explanation. Instead of striking her enemy in the face, as of old, and getting strangled in the dark, Ireland arraigns the oppressor before mankind, and asks the world for a verdict. The passionate one binds her heart into submission, and reasons instead of rebelling. The hottest-blooded race in Europe, not afraid of fighting, God knows, becomes a national exemplar of the supreme force of self-restraint, acceptance, submission, and dependence in the changeless instincts of human nature that must hate wrong when it is made clear and work for justice when it asserts its claim.

JOHN BOYLE O'REILLY.

INTRODUCTION.

To the student of American institutions, the conditions growing out of our diverse populations present great perplexities.

Foreign-born citizens, and those but one generation removed, form an important factor in our educational, industrial and political life.

How our civilization shall assimilate that which is good and discard that which is bad, is the question before the publicist.

Spending about two months in Ireland in the year 1887, I hoped from contact with the people to bring back something of value to the solution of America's problem.

To my interest in the people as related to us was soon added an intense sympathy with their historic struggle for national existence, and their present wretched condition.

This struggle is the latest phase of the universal demand for liberty. In my investigation of the causes which have led to Ireland's present unrest, in addition to a personal study of the situation on the spot, a large number of works written by both Irish and English historians were available, but I felt the need of a summary which would present with as little detail as comprehensiveness and clearness would allow, the strategic points in Ireland's history as affected by English rule. Such

Introduction.

a work I have attempted in the present volume. The substance of the work was prepared on Irish soil, and took the form of letters to the Boston Journal. In its preparation I have consulted a large number of authorities, and have been favored with extended personal interviews with Irish and English statesmen, and with opportunities of listening to debates on pending issues in the English House of Commons.

J. ELLEN FOSTER.

CLINTON, IOWA, *Jan.* 1, 1888.

CONTENTS.

	PAGE
CHAPTER I.	
THE INDICTMENT	7
CHAPTER II.	
DUBLIN CASTLE RULE	19
CHAPTER III.	
EVICTIONS	31
CHAPTER IV.	
LANDLORDISM	44
CHAPTER V.	
POLITICAL DESPOTISM	60
CHAPTER VI.	
INDUSTRIAL DESPOTISM	73
CHAPTER VII.	
COERCION	89
CHAPTER VIII.	
THE IRISH LAND QUESTION	111
CHAPTER IX.	
THE UNION	123
CHAPTER X.	
HOME RULE	135

AUTHORITIES.

Allison. Life of Castlereagh.

Barrington, LL. D., R. C., Sir Jonah. "Rise and Fall of the Irish Nation."

Coote. History of the Union.

Cairnes. Political Essays.

Clancy, John J. Six Months "Unionist's" Rule.

Duffy, Sir C. G. Young Ireland.

Froude. History of England.

Froude. The English in Ireland.

Grattan. Life and Times of Henry Grattan.

Green. History of the English People.

Lecky. The History of England in the Eighteenth Century.

Lecky. Leaders of Public Opinion in Ireland.

McCarthy, Justin. History of our own Times.

Mill, J. S. The Land Question.

O'Brien, W. Smith. Causes of Discontent.

MacNeill, J. G. Swift. How the Union was Carried.

And Speeches, Pamphlets and Documents, by Gladstone, Parnell, Dillon, Harrington, Webb, Redmond, Dawson, Mosely, Fox, Roseberry, Crilly, Leadam and others.

THE CRIME AGAINST IRELAND

CHAPTER I.

THE INDICTMENT.

ALL the world waits with interest the solution of the Irish Question. Ireland's long struggle for constitutional liberty illumines with heroism or disfigures with shame the page of history. Imperial Westminster and gloomy Dublin Castle are both judge and executioner to-day. The former is resplendent with trappings of royalty and the insignia of conscious power, the latter is sullen and dark, and from it the people's heart finds no expression. Its bare walls rise amid the noise of traffic in Dublin streets, where the multitudes pass in decent mien to honest toil, or crowd in rags to beg for bread, or sit in squalor and dumb misery. In sculptured granite the forms of Grattan, O'Brien and

O'Connell still give grim menace to tyranny, and promise morning to Ireland's long night of despair. But while under the shadow of Ireland's wrongs and indignant at England's stupid indifference or criminal complicity with those wrongs, we remember the other oppressions of history. Which among the great nations of the earth may say, "We have not sinned"? Russian Absolutism, Turkish Inhumanity, German Imperialism, French Communism, Spanish Inquisitions and (dear America, thou, too, must hang thy head in shame) African Slavery in the United States — these institutions, whether they be to their peoples the framework of the law, the spirit of the national life, or foul excrescences upon the body politic, all cry out for redress in the supreme court of universal history, and shall find no full discharge till time is no more.

Foremost among these criminal nations to-day stands proud England, world-wide in estate, mighty in resources of material wealth, glorious in literature and arts, unparalleled in achievements, invincible in arms. England must bow her proud head when this

The Indictment.

poor little Ireland — too near for successful resistance, too far for entire assimilation — points in dumb pantomime, or shrieks in wild refrain of race subjugation, of religious oppression, of agrarian outrage and of political despotism.

Has England been so occupied in asserting her military supremacy in the corners of the earth that she fears not this paralysis near her heart?

While developing her wealth in the Indias and the islands of the sea has she forgotten a part of her united kingdom across a narrow channel steadily depopulated by famine, pestilence, and forced emigration, even in sight of her great bounty? Has she carried Bibles to the heathen and herself forgotten the Golden Rule toward her own? Have her scientists discoursed of the origin of species, the orbits of worlds and the distance of suns in arrogant indifference to the Irish peasantry close within her shadow, who in ignorance and misery have toiled in ditching and draining, in sowing and reaping, while they brooded over that anomalous system of Anglo-Irish agrarian economics under which a poor season and failing crops brought starvation and eviction to the tenant, while sun and rain and bountiful harvest enriched him not, but made possible his continuance on the soil, and compelled his payment of increased tribute (rack rent) to a foreign landlord? Has she out of the vitality of a national life nurtured by religious toleration and the spirit of democracy among the people, thrown off one after another the fetters of barbarism and adorned herself with the robes of Christian civilization, while within the breath of her perfumes, the odor of her incense and the sound of her hallelujahs has lain — all full of sores — this Lazarus at the gate?

Have not all the nations of the earth hastened to her jubilee? Have they not from sincere hearts joined her grand Te Deum and Gloria Patria as the procession of half a hundred years has passed in grand review? All voices render unstinted praise to that personal nobility of character in woman, wife, mother, Queen, which has set the name Victoria in the mosaic of this century's achievements. But amid all this glad acclaim I hear

Isaiah's voice: "Is not this the fast that I have chosen, to loose the bonds of wickedness, to undo the heavy burdens and to let the oppressed go free, and that ye break every yoke."

Did the old prophet see Christian England bound to this body of death? I am appalled as I read the page of history and with my own eyes and by personal contact study the distressing condition of the present. The truth compels this terrible arraignment. Would to God it were otherwise!

What is the truth? What does the page of history tell? What are present conditions? And what of the future?

Ireland contains thirty-two thousand square miles. Its shores are circled with mountainous ridges, save where deep sea indentations receive the water of its many rivers. Its soil is productive, and the climate is genial; the gulf stream bears early the moist verdure of the tropics, and stays long the icy hand of winter. The heart of the island is level or gently undulating, and ditching and draining have rescued many bogs. There is now little timber, much having been recklessly wasted, and no re-forestry attempted. With increase of grazing lands there has been little increase in number or quality of cattle, sheep and hogs. Its mineral resources, if any there be, are undeveloped; its great fishing opportunities almost wholly neglected; its manufactories, except only whiskey, porter, linen and a few woollen mills, are extinct. Agricultural products are of the simplest varieties; of rotation of crops little is known. Wheat, barley, oats and the "everlasting potato" are grown on the same field year after year. Potato planting, growing, digging and eating being the simplest co-operative plan between nature and the tiller of the soil, is always approved by the average Irishman, and is by far the most popular combination known in this country.

Why is Ireland thus now a mendicant among the nations? She is not orphaned of Heaven; she is green Erin to her sons: she is still a beautiful island of the sea to every passer-by.

The solution of this sad problem is found

in the dual system of agrarian outrage and military and political despotism forced for centuries upon her, combined with the always operative forces, for good or ill, of race proclivities and ecclesiastical dominance. Ireland's individual history, through association of ideas, is in the minds of uninterested students overshadowed by her political union with England. We are wont to consider English history as including that of Ireland. Not so. One thousand years had made a record not inglorious, before England's attempted conquest, and Ireland's continued rebellion began. The Roman Conquest, that first great mile-stone in England's proud race, marks no time for Ireland. The Roman eagle was never planted on her soil. Her people never felt the imprint of that civilization. When England, deserted by Rome, asked aid of Saxon warriors against the hostile Picts and Scots, Ireland, under its native elective monarchy, the noble kings of the House of Tara, sought no foreign alliance, but by its own valor repelled all invaders, maintained its Celtic race dominance and its national character. England, meanwhile, in exchange for military aid and defence, became Anglo-Saxon in race and government.

During the Saxon period, Ireland and England alike were overrun by Northern marauders. These, sometimes successful in England, never conquered Ireland or deposed her kings. The Danes held a few ports, but not the interior.

Neither was Ireland included in the Norman conquest. England had acknowledged Norman supremacy a hundred years when, in 1170, Henry II began the subjugation of Ireland. And let it be known and remembered in the light of current events that this first invasion of Ireland by England was done under the seal and by the authority of Rome. I quote the words of history: " There was a theory of Christian sovereignty encouraged by Rome and expressed in a bull of Adrian IV, that Ireland and all other islands on which the light of the Gospel of Christ had dawned . . . did of right belong and appertain to St. Peter and the Holy Roman Church."

Henry II had sought and obtained from Pope Adrian IV in 1155, permission "to enter the land of Ireland in order to subdue the people." The first conquest of Ireland was undisputed, but incomplete. Henry set up in Ireland the feudal system introduced into England by William the Conqueror. The land which before was held by tribal tenure he divided among the English colonists whom he settled in Ireland to maintain English supremacy there. The tribal possessors of the soil were victims of military disinheritance of which the so-called constitutional legal processes of the present day are the branded offspring. From that day to this Ireland's griefs have been chiefly caused by England's stupid forgetfulness or willful violation of God's command, " Thou shalt not muzzle the ox that treadeth out the corn." England also attempted to transplant her judicial system; she established courts, she proclaimed legal processes. To these her English colonists might flee for protection, but from them her Irish subjects were debarred and could gain no redress, though they sought it long and bitterly. The tribal system of laws was sufficient under conditions of land ownership and tribal rule, but land tenures broken, foreign possessors in actual or — worse yet — constructive possession, that former system was wholly inadequate. Here again do we see England's oppression of Ireland; claiming to "do equity" she establishes a judicial system which in its very nature makes solemn mockery of even-handed justice.

Assuming to administer government in Ireland according to the people's will, a Parliament was in due time established, with show of representative powers; but the utterances of this Parliament were in the main adulations of suppliant slaves, or the mutterings of automatic hirelings. Of these two systems — judicial and political — the "Castle Rule" of to-day is the lineal descendant. Through the centuries of England's dominance in Ireland she has maintained the same general features: Inequality in political representation, injustice in judicial administration, outrage in land tenure, and coercion everywhere and always. To this has been added the cruel sting of fickleness, of uncertainty in policy. Sometimes by temporary and partial grants of constitutional liberty she has sought to develop strength among the people, with social order and material progress in the state ; but soon, disappointed at lack of immediate and intelligent appreciation and commensurate acceptance of the reciprocal obligations of established government, she has impatiently thrown away even the semblance of that responsible power which alone can command permanent respect in civilized society. She did not in herself possess power enough to long continue that high moral tension, that subornation of brute force necessary to the highest form of just government; and, with strange inconsistency, she has at times wearied of the cost of sustained military occupancy. She has assumed to rule, but has allowed meanwhile an ignorant, superstitious and starving people to consume itself in intestine broils, in agrarian warfare, in religious exterminations and race feuds. The smoke of these contests smelling to heaven has settled on England's proud escutcheon and soiled her illumined record among the nations of the earth.

The England of to-day stands before

these accumulations of the years. Its Tory Government, represented by Lord Salisbury, Prime Minister, Mr. Balfour, Chief Secretary for Ireland, and Lord Londonderry, Lord Lieutenant for Ireland, will be judged by the brain and heart of the English people, aroused as it never has been before, in behalf of Ireland's wrongs; according as they deal with her, will they receive sentence.

This question takes precedence of all others in popular thought; it absorbs all others in the nation's heart. This generation is not responsible for the sins of its ancestors, but this generation must reap what others have sown. The operation of this law is as inevitable concerning nations as with individuals; its results are inexorable in ethics as they are universal in nature.

CHAPTER II.

DUBLIN CASTLE RULE.

ENGLAND boasts that her people enjoy the highest form of constitutional liberty. She points to hoary precedents of asserted and sustained popular sovereignty; to her Magna Charta and Bills of Rights, which guarantee free speech, free press and the right of trial by jury. The government of Ireland by Castle Rule brands this boast as a pitiful sham. British subjects in Ireland, impoverished by eviction acts, emasculated by arms acts, driven by coercion acts, manacled by crimes bills, buried by habeas corpus suspension, menaced by constabulary enlargement, mocked by peace preservation acts, seek in vain for "ancient bulwarks" of English liberty. William O'Brien, M. P.,* (who has but just now completed his sentence as a political prisoner) with a desperation born of patriotism, defied

* The arrest and trial of Wm. O'Brien illustrates the practical working of Dublin Castle authority, and is for that reason referred to.

the hordes of petty tyrants, and declared, by press and speech, the constitutional rights of tillers of the soil.

This horde of tyrants, hid in legal and judicial barracks of temporary power, silence his free speech, threaten his free press, and he, charged with high crime, is denied trial by a jury of his peers.

O, Liberty! what crimes are committed in thy name.

By what authority were proceedings commenced against Mr. O'Brien? By authority of Dublin Castle, exercised through a district inspector having immediate control of armed constabulary. What is Dublin Castle? It is the seat of the local government of Ireland. This government is vested in a privy council, made up of appointees and certain privileged classes. Its executive officers are a Chief Secretary and a Lord Lieutenant. The present incumbents are Mr. Arthur Balfour and Lord Londonderry. This English gentleman (Mr. Balfour) was appointed more especially to carry out the provisions of the Crimes Bill, he being known to be in sympathy with the policy of coercion.

Dublin Castle Rule. 21

They are assisted by fifteen ex-chief secretaries (English), fifteen noblemen, from dukes to lords (the most hated men in Ireland), two past and one present commander of the thirty thousand British soldiers in Ireland. The Prince of Wales and the Lord Chancellor, with judges and law officers of the Crown, complete this strangely constituted "Government for Ireland." The privy council, however, never really meets for serious business; a few members assemble in a back room in the Castle to register and endorse the decrees of the Lord Lieutenant who is himself the mouth-piece of Mr. Balfour.

The above-named legal gentlemen are supposed to advise when, and under what forms of law, to order ordinary or summary proceedings against obnoxious individuals or associations. They may even sit as judges (the present law officials cannot, but most of the judges are ex-Law officers — one of them the ex-Attorney General of the present Government) on first trial or final appeal in the very cases instituted by themselves. It will be seen that not a man of this "Government" is a representative of the people or responsible to them. This is a modern Star Chamber. Its deliberations are with closed doors and its members are sworn to secrecy. By its authority William O'Brien was arrested.

Before whom was he cited to appear on preliminary examination?

Before resident magistrates of the town where, as member of Parliament, he had addressed his constituents on local interests. These magistrates are not the people's servants, elected by them and responsible to them, but elected by Dublin Castle, and accountable to that power alone for the manner in which they conduct examinations of its political opponents. Their appointment and salary are both largely dependent on the uncontrolled good pleasure of the Lord Lieutenant, and for tenure of office and promotion he is absolutely dependent on the Government.

On what testimony was Mr. O'Brien's arrest ordered?

On the testimony of certain Castle officials.

Dublin Castle Rule. 23

By whom was he ordered to jail to await trial?

By a Dublin Castle magistrate sitting at Cork.

Before whom will he be tried?

Not by a jury of his peers selected from the county where his alleged offence was committed, but by two magistrates appointed by Dublin Castle and making returns to it.

It is in their power, under forms of law, to deprive him of his liberty and to commit him to hard labor for a term of six months, if they and their superiors at Dublin Castle shall deem it expedient so to do.

If the sentence shall be for a term of more than one month, he has the right to appeal to the Court at Quarter Sessions. This tribunal is instituted by the same Castle power, and differs from the former only in number of magistrates sitting. In no event can this British subject be tried by a jury of his peers. Shocking as is this illustration of Castle Rule, it portrays but one feature of the galling despotism under which Ireland groans. Every department of public administration feels the blight.

As set forth in a speech of Mr. Chamberlain, M. P., just before he became a so-called Unionist: "It is a system which is founded on the bayonets of thirty thousand soldiers encamped permanently as in a hostile country. It is a system as completely centralized and bureaucratic as that with which Russia governs Poland, or as that which was common in Venice under Austrian rule. An Irishman at this moment cannot move a step, he cannot lift a finger in any parochial, municipal or educational work, without being confronted, interfered with, or controlled by, an English official appointed by a foreign Government, and without a shadow or shade of representative authority. I say the time has come to reform altogether the absurd and irritating anachronism which is known as Dublin Castle; to sweep away altogether these alien boards of foreign officials, and to substitute for them a genuine Irish administration for purely Irish business."

The essential feature of a representative government is that the people shall be governed by laws made and administered by representatives elected by them and responsible to them. Majorities settle who these representatives shall be. The Parliament of Great Britain, through its working arm — the House of Commons — thus governs England and Scotland. The "Government" is composed of ministers selected by the Crown, but approved by the people and responsible to them. The present Chief Secretary for Ireland was thus chosen, but not from the people of Ireland, and not responsible to them. This Chief Secretary, the Lord Lieutenant who is also appointed by the Government, live in Dublin; these two are practically governors of Ireland; the under officials who manipulate details of administration are largely a permanent body, their tenures of office being continually strengthened by the indolent indifference of irresponsible governors. Three bodies known as the "Big Boards" cover the larger part of Ireland's domestic affairs; the Local Government Board, the Board of Works, the Board of National Education. Every member of every one of these boards is nominated by the Lord Lieutenant and wholly irresponsible to the Irish people or their representatives in Parliament.

The first board has supervision of the poor funds, the public health, the pollution of rivers, the diseases of cattle, and other purely local matters. It even exercises control in the constitution of new town boards, as to the number of members of these boards, and may refuse to approve details of local expenditure, and by sealed orders dismiss and dissolve boards according to its own pleasure.

The Board of Works exercises great powers and extensive operations. It is wholly under control of the Lord Lieutenant, its three members being nominated by him. It directs construction of public works and the management of harbors and public parks. Minor local boards having nominally some little power are really subservient to it, because it controls the expenditure of money, and may withhold at its own option. The proceedings of this Board of Works have repeatedly been censured in the House of Commons by large majorities of the Irish members, but with no avail.

English and Scotch members find it easier to uphold Dublin Castle than to become individually informed of local Irish affairs.

So also with the Board of National Education. No department of the nation's life lies so near its heart as the education of its children. None could with more safety be entrusted with the people themselves. This board of twenty members, prescribing school regulations, selecting or making schoolbooks, engaging and controlling teachers, is nominated by this ubiquitous Lord Lieutenant. One very noticeable feature of the anti-national character of this so-called National Board is the absence of materials in the text books out of which to grow a national spirit. The prevailing tone and conduct of these schools does not nurture patriotism. The heroic in Ireland's history, being set in the frame of English despotism, must not forsooth be taught the children. But, notwithstanding all these prejudicial limitations, the national school is Ireland's greatest boon and is working out her redemption. England comprehends too slowly for her peace, that which all tyrants must sooner or later learn, that the alphabet and the multiplication table are universal emancipators.

Not only are Ireland's materialities administered by the Castle, but its public charities, asylums for lunatics, prison boards and boards of charities and bequests. So also the first circles of organized government, the county, the township and the municipal corporations are under Castle scrutiny.

Grand juries of the counties and resident magistrates are directly appointed by the Lord Lieutenant, and are generally of the landed, titled class, or their family dependents.

To pay the salaries of these officials the tenant is taxed. Before inquisitions thus created and sustained he may be cited if charged with little or great offences; from petty larceny and malicious mischief to felonies and high treason.

These judicial functions are exercised under statutes enacted by Parliament for the United Kingdoms of Great Britain and Ireland; but for a century these statutes have been so warped or distorted by exceptional

Dublin Castle Rule.   29

legislation for Ireland, known as Crimes and Coercion Acts, that but little semblance of original justice remains. Municipalities like Dublin and Cork wear trappings and the suits of power, which are but fictitious tinsel; for here and everywhere the Castle is in many matters ultimate authority.

This is in bare outline the autonomy of the Castle system; to follow its ramifications would require a microscopical study of the entire life of the people.

This despotism can only be sustained by force. This ever-present force is an armed constabulary of twelve thousand men sustained by thirty thousand troops of Her Majesty's regular army.

The people of Ireland, by act of Parliament, are disarmed; their miserable huts are continually searched lest an ambitious youth should by any means have secreted the hereditary fowling-piece or the modern firearms. In the midst of the huts, in the village or on the mountain side, is seen the substantial Government police barrack, where well clothed, well fed, fully armed men drill in the use of defensive and offensive weapons.

So, also, amid the plain attire of the few well-to-do and the many ragged of the native population is conspicuous the bright red coat of the regular British soldier or the national attire of the Scotch fusileer. One cannot walk the streets an hour without these visible signs of England's conquest and Ireland's subjection.

This is not a mere tale of to-day. It has been continued through many generations, and is a principal factor in Ireland's present degradation.

CHAPTER III.

EVICTIONS.

SINCE the tenth century Ireland has been the seat of wars of conquest and the scene of intestine strife, unparalleled in the history of warfare, in intensity and atrocity if not in territorial area. Weapons of warfare have changed with the centuries. A contemporary writer says of this people, "They are soldiers from birth."

The conflict is as irrepressible to-day as at any period in the past; the weapons now used are fit for the occasion and invented by its necessities; there are preparations for an immediate charge all along the line; there are provisions for an unlimited siege.

In their present resistance to the measures of tyranny the tenants carry a flag bearing the simple words "Plan of Campaign." The landlords through summary proceedings peculiar to the Irish system, aided by provisions of the penal code framed for their special benefit, and sustained by Crown officials, armed constabulary and even Her Majesty's troops, begin the assault. A war between these two contending factions is waged before the gaze of the world; if to-day a jury were impaneled from the Christian nations, a verdict would be given for Ireland and against her dual oppressors — landlordism and political despotism. Peaceable, law-abiding people in England and America watch the struggle with sympathy for the tenant in his deliberate and systematic resistance to the execution of law. Gentle and refined women cheer the resistants and do honor to the man — John Dillon — whose brain formulated the plan, and to the great orator, William O'Brien, whose impassioned words inspire the combatants to "stand firm," and to "make no surrender." Statesmen, representing the clearest brain and the stoutest moral sense of two hemispheres, are proud to receive as brother-patriots a host of others, captains of fifties and captains of hundreds, who lead the people of Ireland in this their desperate struggle. The names of Davitt, of O'Neil, of Harrington, of Condon, of

Evictions.   33

Clancy, of Healy, of the brothers Manderville, will swell the record of heroes who loved their country and thought it all honor to suffer for her sake. These, all under Parnell, commander-in-chief, form a well-disciplined army, hardened by long exposure, drilled in many combats and inspired by real patriotism.

What is the cause of the war? "What do they kill each other for?" There are in Ireland hundreds of farm tenants who cannot pay their rent; some of them have been in arrears for years. The landlord desires to receive that which is, in law, his due. The tenants are utterly unable to pay. The landlord serves upon these delinquents certain legal notices and orders them through forms of law to leave their premises. The tenants refuse to go. The landlord says they shall, and brings to his aid armed policemen and even the regular troops. Herein is the resistance. Here comes the tug of war. Let us watch one of the many engagements of this campaign.

Within a stone and turf fence lie seventy acres of tolerable farm land, except fourteen

of it, which is low and in wet seasons under
water. It is tilled in small patches of corn,
barley, oats and potatoes. It was stony, but
now pretty well cleared; it is enriched by
sand and seaweed washed up in storms and
gathered in inclement seasons from the
strand. A few sheep and cows add their
treasure of daily food and winter covering.
The dwelling-house is of stone and mortar;
the out-houses of similar construction and
appearance. For centuries this tenant and
his ancestors have tilled this very spot of
earth. They have drained the bogs, picked
the stone, built the dwelling, the out-houses,
the fences; have put upon it every trace of
cultivation which it bears. The present
tenant, during his forty years' occupancy as
head of a family, has expended eleven hundred pounds in improvements. On this
"holding" the rent has been several times
raised, and that in proportion as through the
tenant's labor and expenditure the property
has increased in value. Now the tenant pays
an annual rental of eighty-four pounds. In
good years, and when produce commanded
good prices, the landlord's claim was met,

but since 1879 have come bad years, falling prices, and the amount of rental has not been realized off the farm; one half year's rent is due and unpaid. There also hangs over this holding a "hanging gale," that term being applied to an arrears of one half year's rent which accrued many years ago, beyond the lifetime of the present tenant. This arrears might have been paid in good years, but was refused by the landlord, the last refusal being some sixteen years ago. This is a common form of oppression; the landlord can evict without notice when a year's rent is due. Thus the "hanging gale" and the half year's present indebtedness make the required "pound of flesh." This one year's rental is all that is unpaid on this seventy acres, and for this the tenant is served with the ejectment writ.

In the legends which this family tells, as by glowing peat fires on the hearth they sit of winter nights, you will find that their distant ancestor was a proud chief amid his clan; that the acres all about were his and theirs; that cornfields waved; that cattle grazed upon the mountain side and in the glens, until, on an evil day there came proud strangers in the dress of men-of-war. They will tell you that, though the men fought hard and long, they were at last overcome and lost their land; many died of sword and famine and pestilence, but of the few who survived their ancestor was one; he and his, through changing fortunes under many kings retained these few acres, and from them gathered sustenance enough to live and rear the generations that have been worn out on this soil; but now, alas! poor crops, falling prices and lessened remittances from America have all conspired, and he cannot pay his required tribute to the titled owner, who never expended one dollar on the land, but received it as an inheritance of conquest and confiscation.

Even-handed justice declares this tenant has a claim upon the acres which he has tilled; the resistance which he makes to this eviction writ is based upon this sense of justice.

Under the Plan of Campaign systematic resistance was planned; windows, sashes and frames are taken out; against these openings iron gates, taken from lanes on the farm, are placed on the inside and braced by logs as big as a man's body; these window props and those against the doors are secured by iron spikes driven in the earth floor; grindstones, anvils, pieces of farm implements are useful; blackthorn branches and limbs of trees, weapons in themselves, serve as improvised barricades. Every door and window having been secured with sufficient strength to resist any lesser charge than from mounted cannon, the inside space is filled with dense masses of brush and briers, which is woven through and bound about with wires.

In houses containing separate apartments each is similarly arranged, and one or two men sleep in the house at night, when a "charge" is anticipated. They are supplied with rations of food and weapons of war, sticks, pitchforks, "blackthorns," hot water, hives of bees, red pepper and sulphur for smoking out chimneys if approach is attempted from that quarter. Sometimes the women occupants are left inside as the most vigorous defenders.

This is a barricaded house under the Plan

of Campaign. Its defences and appliances are varied according to the ingenuity and the resources of the tenant and those who aid him. Perhaps the words "Plan of Campaign" are conspicuously painted on the outside as a signal of defiance; outrage and conscious right make men very bold. This house is approached by the authorities with an ejectment writ. The sheriff and perhaps two deputies first demand admission; no answer received; then begins the forceful assault; he orders up his "emergency men," eight or ten supporters popularly known as the "crowbar brigade." They carry picks, axes, crowbars, and use them with what effect they can. They are protected by constables with batons and swords, and sometimes armed companies of the regular troops. The contending parties are not alone in these battles; the people gather from miles around; the news spreads like wildfire; for the battle of one tenant is the cause of all. It not unfrequently happens that insulting language is used by constables and bystanders, and assault and injury and sometimes killing ensues. Dublin Castle, not long ago, sent official instructions in the " don't hesitate to shoot" message which has become a notorious phrase in street parlance.

The presence of sick or aged in the house do not deter these evictors. It is in evidence that death has occurred on the roadside before tottering age could find a shelter. One tenant sorrowfully tells how he gathered his family under the roof of a kindly neighbor, but was obliged the very next day to go to the town for a coffin for his dead mother.

A clergyman states that he administered the rites of the Church to a poor woman so near death she could not be moved; the roof was taken from the house over her head while she was in the unconscious state preceding death, and when she passed away there was only a winnowing sheet between her and the blue vault above. Houses are unroofed to prevent the return of the homeless wanderers. Sometimes they are burned to make assurance doubly sure.

See the mournful procession at the roadside, on the highway, mad with rage, frenzied with grief, or dumb with despair. Old men, little children, women with babes in arms or great with child, are there: the tenant, his family, the laborers and their families, perhaps a dozen, perhaps two dozen souls. These must find shelter among a population but little better off than themselves, or go to the poor house, or die by the roadside or in the sheltering ditch. The tale is so dreadful Christian credulity can scarce receive it, but "seeing is believing." And this has been going on for years. During the last five years the Inspector General of Constabulary estimates over fifty-seven thousand persons to have been thus dispossessed. Within the fifty years of Victoria's reign not less than four millions have been by these "forms of law" turned from their homes.

What is the final result? Which side wins? Usually the landlord, aided by the Government; the statistics given show it; unroofed houses, burned-down houses, untenanted farms everywhere testify, and the depopulation of the country confirms it. In former years there was little substantial resistance; entreaties, tears, frenzied appeals, hastily improvised defences were no barrier to the evicting force. Hundreds were sometimes driven out in a single day. Mr. Gladstone in 1870 said, "We have made ejectments cheap and easy, and notices to quit have descended upon the people like snowflakes." But the combat has changed; the success of the landlord is now difficult, dangerous and expensive. Mr. William O'Brien, in the Mitchelstown speech for which he was imprisoned, urged the people, through deliberate, systematic resistance by the Plan of Campaign, to "make evictions as slow and as expensive to the Government as possible."

Evictions fall now and then; they are still hard as hailstones, but they are not "cheap and easy"; they are not "thick as snowflakes." There are hundreds of houses in Ireland so barricaded that it would take months of continued siege with thousands of armed men in the midst of a hostile country to accomplish the undertaking.

The people are, with few exceptions, in direct antagonism to the police and their attempt at enforcement. Much annoyance is attempted. Taverns will not lodge them;

car drivers will not carry them; they are avoided in the streets as if infected with disease. They are jeered at by the pestiferous "small boy" and sneered at by the saucy girl; old women utter imprecations when they pass; and in one instance a whole congregation left the church when a few entered to attend mass. The clergy, mostly Catholics, are in sympathy and constant co-operation with the resistance. They are at evictions directing the orderly proceedings of these emergency gatherings. They have in some instances been imprisoned for refusing to testify of Plan of Campaign proceedings of which they had knowledge through their professional relations. One highly esteemed and greatly honored priest, Canon Keller of Youghall, was thus imprisoned.

Evictions are a well-known procedure under all systems of law; they are not peculiar to Irish administration; but the system of land tenures, landlordism and immemorial usage is peculiar. Under systems of injustice which philanthropy and religion have been blind to, and economy and statesmanship were deaf to, the tenant has been ground between the millstone of the landlord's avarice and his own necessities. The accumulations of the years have left before him a mass of tyrannies and murderous conditions through which he must fight his way or die. He chooses to fight.

CHAPTER IV.

LANDLORDISM.

THE American student of the Irish agrarian question will fail to comprehend the situation from a legislative, political or humanitarian aspect until he becomes acquainted with Ireland's historical grievances and her unwritten law which custom has established from "time out of mind."

The conflict waged for centuries can be traced to three fundamental wrongs; conquest and confiscation, race and creed animosities, landlord absenteeism. These are the questions which the American philanthropist must study; this is the problem which the English statesman must solve.

England's conquests of Ireland began under Henry II about the year 1170. He set up the system of land tenure which had been introduced into England by the Nor-

Landlordism. 45

mans a hundred years before. The nominal title to the land was taken from the Irish and parcelled out to Englishmen. Such of the original possessors as were not slain in battle hid in the forests and hills, and returned under their unconquered chiefs to contend for the soil lately their own, and to settle again upon estates vacated by English colonists who became wearied with the continual defence of their newly acquired lands. In many cases the English lords made common cause with the native population and were in their turn proscribed as traitors who had become "Hibernis ipsis Hiberniosis." For centuries a nominal supremacy was maintained, varied often, and in different sections of the island, by raids and rebellions, as succeeding kings attempted with more or less severity to maintain England's authority. No apology was made for this wholesale confiscation; the right of might was sufficient warrant.

Yet at the beginning of the Tudor line the disgraceful incompetence of the Dublin government and the utter neglect of the authorities in London had resulted in a state of things in which the nominal "pale" of English sovereignty was limited to the immediate neighborhood of Dublin, while some of the great towns of the South were left actually to engage in private war.

Elizabeth in her reign, and Cromwell in his protectorate, entered afresh on wars of conquest and confiscation; the later, known as the Cromwellian Settlement, exceeded all its predecessors in the amount and extent of the desolation which followed. Five sixths of the people perished or emigrated. Those who remained fought with exasperation, when they had strength to fight, or by secret organization sought revenge by assassination and fire. The landlords of the present day, whose names have become familiar through tales of recent evictions and present state of siege, hold their titles by a chain welded through centuries on these anvils of conquest and confiscation. The Ponsonby estate at Youghall, Cork County, illustrates this. The section of country now included in the counties of Waterford and Cork was part of a grant given by Elizabeth to Sir Walter Raleigh:

the house where he lived, the yew-trees under which he smoked Indian tobacco (much to the terror of his servant) are still to be seen and are often visited by the tourist. From this proud knight of the Virgin Queen the land passed to the great Earl of Cork, and from him to the ancestors of the present owner, Charles William Talbot Ponsonby.

It is recorded that England's first conquest of Ireland was at the instigation of Pope Adrian IV, who, in pursuance of the theory of Christian sovereignty encouraged by Rome, claimed that "all lands upon which the Gospel of Christ had dawned did of right belong to the holy Roman Church." Henry II, not adverse to conquest for its own sake, availed himself of this added authority, and waged his wars in the name of the faith.

When, however, England at the Reformation became Protestant, Ireland still adhered to Rome, and the struggle to maintain English dominance was aided by the mockery of religious propaganda. The slaughter of Catholics by the sword, or by inhumanities too revolting to narrate, marked the early stages of this prosecution; later, when humanity sickened with the sight of these rivers of human gore, more indirect and refined processes of extermination were applied. Hallam says of these: " To have exterminated the Catholics by the sword, or expelled them like the Moriscos of Spain, would have been little more repugnant to justice and humanity, but incomparably more politic." Numberless disabilities, educational and industrial, were laid upon Catholics. Queen Anne banished from Ireland all Catholic teachers and sentenced them to death in case of return. Because wealthy persons evaded this law by sending their children to the schools of the Continent this was forbidden under pain of forfeiture of lands to the Crown. A priest, on pain of death, could not marry a Catholic to a Protestant. A Protestant woman who should marry a Catholic forfeited her estate to the next Protestant heir-at-law. Catholics were excluded from the liberal professions, except that of medicine. They could not until the year 1782, acquire landed property. They were disfranchised until 1793. They were ineligible to Parliament until the year 1829. It would be impossible to set forth the magnitude of this oppression or to detail its pettiness. It was met in old times by persecution of the same spirit, though not to the same extent, by Catholic outrages on Protestants, but these are now unknown; in fact the Catholic municipal towns are constantly electing Protestants to the mayoralty and town council, although the converse is rarely true.

The Government has been behind Protestantism; retaliation, revenge and bigotry have been the only intrenchments from which Catholicism could wage its battles.

These ever-present animosities have continually hardened the heart of the Protestant landlord and embittered the feelings of the Catholic tenant. Definite and general attempts to exterminate the Irish race or to drive them from the larger and better portions of the country and to substitute an English and Scotch peasantry, with English laws, English customs and English tenures, were adopted as a settled policy in the reign of Elizabeth. Up to that time an actual possession of the land had satisfied the hungry invader; he was willing it should be tilled by those of the native Irish whose broken spirit and abject condition made them more or less submissive to the conquerors. But English colonists living in detached sections of the country soon found themselves unable to maintain possession under the continual menace of the wandering Irish, who hid in the mountains and still rallied to the call of their chiefs. The only alternative was to exterminate by famine, fire and sword these dangerous people.

The story of this process of extermination is simply horrible.

While Shakespeare and Spenser were making memorable the literature of the Elizabethan era, England's soldiers were filling Ireland with "carcasses and ashes."

In 1576 one Malby, the President of Connaught, made the following official report: —

"At Christmas I marched into their territory [Shan Burke's] and, finding courteous dealing with them had like to have cut my throat, I thought good to take another

Landlordism. 51

course, and so, with determination to consume them with fire and sword, sparing neither old nor young, I entered their mountains. I burnt all their corn and houses, and committed to the sword all that could be found, when were slain at that time above sixty of their best men, and among them the best leaders they had. This was Shan Burke's country. Then I burnt Ulick Burke's country. In like manner I assaulted a castle, when the garrison surrendered. I put them to the misericordia of my soldiers. They were all slain. Thence I went on, sparing none which came in my way, which cruelty did so amaze their followers that they could not tell where to bestow themselves. It was all done in rain and frost and storm, journeys in such weather bringing them the sooner to submission. They are humble enough now, and will yield to any terms we like to offer them."

Is it strange that the descendants of these men, thus persecuted, who have passed the story down from father to son, should hate the name of England; is it any wonder that the peasant who through fire and sword and famine has kept the holding of his fathers, should to the very death resist the writ of eviction and the armed force that executes it?

A quarter of a century later the Lord Deputy writes: " I have often said and written it is famine that must consume the Irish, as our swords and other endeavors worked not that speedy effect which is expected. Hunger would be a better, because a speedier, weapon to employ against them than the sword. I burned all along the lough within four miles of Dungannon and killed one hundred people, sparing none, of what quality, age or sex soever, besides many burned to death. We killed man, woman and child, horse, beast and whatever we could find." While the echo of these terrible words still lingers, hear the cold irony, the heartless comment of the English aristocrat who says, " These Irish are a discontented, disorderly people; they are never satisfied! " But to his haughty highness there comes the thundering answer of the English democracy: " By our help he shall be satisfied; he shall possess the soil he has tilled; he shall build a state and govern it himself. Christian civilization answers, it ought so to be."

More potential in producing hostile relations and distressing conditions than origin of title or race and creed animosities is landlord absenteeism, which has always been an agent of evil in Ireland. Underneath all differences of race or creed or accidents of birth there exists the common human tie which, without active volition on the part of either landlord or tenant, would have bound their common interests.

As dew-drops on the cup of the lily and the leaf of the wayside weed mingle when drawn by the sun to the hanging cloud and return to the earth in blessing, so these human lives if brought within certain radii of influence would have generated through the operation of involuntary laws certain centripetal and centrifugal forces which would have held the solar social system in harmonious operation. But the landlord was beyond the bounds of the system. Humanitarian laws had no chance to do their ameliorating work.

He does not care for Ireland. He values

property there merely as it enables present tenants to pay present rents. He does not live there, nor spend his money there. When the Irish tenant in summer is toiling at ploughing and sowing, mowing and reaping, or ditching and draining, the landlord is in the mountains of Switzerland or at a Continental watering place.

When the tenant in winter — his little crop gathered, his few potatoes dug — is driven by snow and ice under his thatched roof and within his little hut, and when he and his family, and perhaps the faithful donkey, his beast of burden, make common cause in seeking warmth from the glowing peat upon the hearth, the landlord is in Paris or in London spending the money gathered by his resident agent from these poor people. Even the few resident landlords do not make common cause with the people. They live in castles, within wooded domains, surrounded by high walls. These homes are furnished with great luxury, but not as Irish growth. The carpets, the furniture, the pictures, the books, the wardrobe, the tailor, the dressmaker, the bootmaker, the milliner — these are French or English, almost never Irish. Even family servants are often brought from beyond the channels.

The money actually taken out of the country by this absenteeism is enormous. It is estimated to be at present about six million pounds per annum. Think what this would do in internal improvements, in industrial or mercantile investment! The number of absentees at the present time is estimated to be nearly eight thousand.

If the individual energy of these men owning more than one half of the arable land of Ireland were applied in public enterprises, what an impetus would be given its material prosperity. If the personal moral influence of these gentlemen of education and leisure were felt in educational and philanthropic culture, how much more elevated might the social tone become.

Absenteeism has always been Ireland's curse. The early kings desired to prevent it by compulsory legislation. Residence was required for certain periods in each year, and increased taxes were required of absentees. These coercive measures were of little effect beyond that of collecting a few pounds revenue, and the whole attempted remedy was a legislative farce.

It is significant that rack-renting and evictions have, with a few exceptions, been most common and distressing on the estates of absentees.

Mr. Froude, who is not by any means an Irish partisan, says of this unnatural system under which Ireland has long groaned: —

"The absentee landlords of Ireland had neither community of interest with the people nor sympathy of race. They had no fear of provoking their resentment, for they lived beyond their reach. They had no desire for their welfare, for as individuals they were ignorant of their existence. They regarded their Irish estates as the sources of their income; their only desire was to extract the most out of them which the soil could be made to yield; and they cared no more for the souls and the bodies of those who were in fact committed to their charge than the owners of a West Indian plantation for the herds of slaves whose backs were blistering in the cane fields."

Landlordism. 57

Out of these confiscations, animosities and absenteeisms, has grown up by custom and English law a landlord and tenant code, wholly differing in spirit, indeed, a complete inversion of that which prevails elsewhere. Improvements, such as dwelling houses, farm buildings, fences, draining and the like, are in England and America built by the landlord; there is also an implied covenant that these betterments shall be kept in needed repair at his expense; shall be replaced by him if burned or otherwise destroyed.

In Ireland the tenant makes all improvements; the landlord does nothing. The tenant builds at his own cost, and keeps in repair the dwelling, the outhouses, the fences, etc.

This has been the custom since the times of confiscation, when the lands were given to Englishmen who, rather than live in Ireland and care for the booty given by a conquering invader, left the estates in possession of native Irish peasants, being satisfied to obtain what income they could from that which cost them nothing.

As the tenant, impelled by the necessities of existence, improved the farm from time to time, the rent was raised proportionately. It is admitted by all intelligent judges that landlords in Ireland receive greater rent for farms improved by tenants than English and Scotch landlords receive for farms improved by themselves.

The landlords of Ireland have received more actual rent money for the last ten years than the value of the amount of produce raised off the land. The children and other relatives in America have sent large sums to the old folks at home to pay the landlord's claim, and the father and sons of the family have worked in the mines or other industries of England and Wales and earned the money to pay for the poor shelter of the little holding.

Not only does the Irish landlord receive unconscionable rents, but is aided by special legislation in collecting it; he may evict his tenant for non-payment by a summary proceeding peculiar to the Irish system. He is further aided by a penal code with provisions framed for his special benefit; he may without the intervention of any court call to his assistance officers of the Crown, armed constabulary, and even Her Majesty's regular troops. Such is Irish landlordism; base and wicked in inception, oppressive and merciless in continuance, murderous in results.

CHAPTER V.

POLITICAL DESPOTISM.

POLITICAL despotism is the great conspirator in the crime against Ireland. It stands indicted with landlordism, oppressive taxation, industrial death, religious persecution, chronic insurrection, and is itself the assassin of constitutional liberty.

England's early supremacy in Ireland was sustained by force. She employed the sword, fire, famine and common butchery. She drove the native Irish into the most sterile parts of the country, and kept them there on pain of death. "To Hell or Connaught" was the shibboleth of that barbaric age.

The beautiful Shannon, in its circling course to the sea, became a dead-line to the fugitives. When the thirst for conquest had been assuaged by surfeit of slaughter, and the people of England had secured for themselves more clearly defined constitutional powers, the form of despotism in Ireland changed. There was not less despotism; its modes were more refined, though not less oppressive. The philanthropic endeavors of friends of Ireland in the British Parliament did from time to time attempt remedial legislation of tenant wrongs; but despotism personified in landed aristocracy usually strangled these attempts. Very few of the many bills introduced ever become laws. Between the tenant and needed relief appeared the ever-present intervener. The land bills recently enacted, presumably in the interest of the tenant, contain provisions somewhat equitable; but it is not every one who can comply with their conditions and is able to bear the expense of the land court; thus the larger number of those most needing relief are unable to secure the advantages of the bills. A commission was instituted to sit as a court and to fix a "judicial rent."

This commission was appointed by Dublin Castle, and is said to have been largely made up of its political partisans, the landlord class or their dependents. It soon appeared that the administration of the law was in the interest of the landlord, not of the tenant. The commission made its reductions on the basis of the clearly proved estimate that the land had not produced even in good times the value of the old rents. These rents had been met mainly by moneys received from Irish emigrants in America. Lord Dufferin states that sum to have been upward of thirteen million pounds between the years 1848 and 1864.

During recent years remittances directly to tenants for the payment of rent have largely decreased. A more intelligent and effective means of aiding the Irish cause than supporting English landlords by the payment of exorbitant rents has been devised.

An illustration of this, and of the devotion of Irish children to the old folks at home, recently came to our knowledge. A lad left County Cork for Boston ten years ago. He worked at his trade — harness-making — and regularly sent to his father for rent money twenty pounds a year. On a recent visit to the place of his birth he found the old man in the same wretched hut, in poverty and rags. Every shilling of the two hundred pounds he had sent had gone into the landlord's coffers. With an oath, registered in the just court of heaven, he said: "Father, I'll take care of you, but the landlords of Ireland shall never have another dollar of my hard earnings." There was one more eviction, and then the old man went with his sturdy son to America. This failure of supplies from America, and the universal decrease in agricultural values, combined at the same time to render tenants even more unable to pay the reduced rent than they had been to satisfy the former more exorbitant demand of the landlord. Of many a tenant might it be said, "the last state of that man was worse than the first." The land bill of the year 1887 has as yet (January, 1888) made no record; from it the tenant hopes little, because the commission, already appointed, originated from and is responsible to Dublin Castle. Evictions are still the order of the day, and the tenant's "holding" is as precarious as ever. There is a significance almost pathetic in the term denoting a tenant's occupancy.

It is not his "farm," his "estate," his "place," his "ranch," it is his "holding." He does not take root as does the tree or garden shrub; he "holds" like an ivy to the wall, a lichen to the rock; he clings as do these prolific natives of his Emerald Isle.

An Irishman's love of hearth and home and country is the strongest passion of his nature; the landlord has traded upon it.

It is told of one of these, a poor old fellow, who had reared a large family upon a little patch, and was reduced to turnips and salt as their only food, that when urged to send his oldest sons to America, with the prospect of soon following himself when better times came to them, he answered with spirit, " No ; I'll never go; isn't this my home; wasn't I born here and my fathers before me ? I'll eat turnips while I have them, and then I'll live on the flower of the furze; but I'll never leave: I'll die here as my fathers did." This man had only a " holding," for which he paid an annual rental of over a pound an acre; he and his fathers had wrested from the soil and gathered by labor in other places this tribute to the landlord's greed; but they had no deed or lease, only a " holding."

A German publicist, endeavoring to find a word in his own tongue to express the peculiar disabilities of the Irish tenant-at-will on his holding, said, " Why not call him ' the hunt-off-able ? ' " (Wegjagdbau.) This tenant in America might claim the rights of a squatter sovereign; in Ireland he is the victim of squatter serfdom. The intention of Parliament in the recent land bills was doubtless good, though weakened by the administration of Dublin Castle, and further compromised by contemporaneous coercion acts. While the tenant is being invited to Dublin Castle Land Court, from Dublin Castle issues proclamation after proclamation assailing the right of free speech and public meeting, and summons after summons of arrest of Irish patriots. It denies to these the constitutional right of trial by jury, and by summary proceedings consigns them to the felon's cell.

While with one hand it offers the olive branch of a doubtful land bill, with the right hand of its power it arms fourteen thousand constabulary to assist the landlord in evictions for non-payment of arrears impossible to meet. As they "remember Mitchelstown" (according to Mr. Gladstone's appeal) their dimmed eyes can scarcely see the olive branch. The presence of an armed constabulary is a constant reminder that they are subjects of a foreign Government, in spirit if not in fact; this becomes the more exasperating when they find out that they are taxed an enormous sum to support this constabulary, whose chief service is to enforce the claims of absent English landlords.

In a certain area of less than ten miles square, in a quiet section of the country containing less than ten thousand people, this expense to the rate payers of Great Britain and Ireland is over sixty thousand pounds per year. England should remember that one of the grievances which caused her the loss of the American colonies was that she quartered soldiers upon the people in time of peace. Is it likely that her subjects a century later will bear without aggressive protest this quarterage upon their rent rolls?

The political despotism of the present will do well to steer clear of these landmarks of history.

Two centuries ago Ireland's wool and linen manufactories formed no inconsiderable part of her resources. These, with exports of cattle and sheep, threatened materially to compete with like industries in the English market. Here again political despotism becomes an intervener in the interest of English capitalists and against Irish subjects. By definite and sweeping acts of Parliament in restraint of Irish trade and commerce the growing industries of Ireland were destroyed.

Not only did despotism make itself felt in materialities, it sought to lay an embargo on the consciences of men. Civil and political disabilities were laid upon Catholics, and religious persecution even unto death was authorized under forms of law. Not till the time of the present generation has there been the same toleration of religious opinion in Ireland as in England. That Ireland has been for many years in a state of chronic insurrection cannot be denied. The massacres of 1641 and of 1798 stain the page of history; the record of young Ireland, of Phœnix Clubs, of Fenian raids, of Land Leagues are inseparably interwoven in the history of the country. The careful student can not, however, fail to discover that these movements were the results of pre-existing conditions; they were not the cause of those conditions. Whenever the work of secret organizations matured in breaches of the peace there had been immediate or proximate assaults, real or supposed, from a despotic government.

The British Government has seemed blind to the political truth, that free discussion and untrammeled organization for redress of grievances are the necessary safety valves of public order. By repressive and despotic class legislation it has become *particeps criminis* in numerous social outbreaks, until now by the grim irony of retributive justice England finds the path of her own progress impeded by a mass of rubbish, accumulated from the injustice of centuries, and is obliged to set herself to a careful consideration of the equities in Ireland's cause.

Her House of Commons sat for months in controversy over the details of coercion measures to the utter suspension of Imperial legislation. England, Scotland and Wales in the name of their neglected interests protest; protesting for themselves and for their own interests, they have come to study the whole question from the broad plane of philanthropic statesmanship. The realization comes with force to many of their clearest thinkers, that the present Tory Government by its coercive policy in Ireland is establishing a precedent of violence to constitutional rights, as threatening to English liberty in the future as it is outrageous and insulting to Irish Nationalism by its recent exercise in the trial and conviction of William O'Brien. It would be impossible to believe Christian England knowingly guilty of Irish outrages in legislation and administration, except by considering the nation as consisting of two independent and sometimes antagonistic elements — the English people and the English Government.

The English people are true to the common instincts of humanity; they love justice, they mean to do equity ; but they themselves have not been long self-governed, and have been absorbed in reform measures pertaining to their own economic grievances. The extension of the franchise to its present limits is very recent, and is still much incumbered. The spirit of aristocracy is the same everywhere; it has been bridled in England; it has taken the bit in its teeth in Ireland. The masses of the people who now rise under the majestic name — English Democracy — have only lately had power to materially influence governmental policy; they have known little of that policy in the sister country, from which they were separated by stormy channels, and by difference of race and creed. The English Government, as distinguished from the English people, has been obliged to sustain its policy of conquest by further acts of confiscation and coercion, or to retire from the possession of the island, or to give to the people some such form of independent local government as is outlined in Mr. Gladstone's Home Rule measure. The Tory Government, on its own account and for its own peace, would doubtless set

Political Despotism. 71

the island adrift; but the integrity of the Empire would not allow that; it hesitates to give a local government with greater powers than England, Scotland and Wales possess or ask; it talks in grandiloquent phrase about the " integrity of the Empire " being endangered by Ireland's demands, and fills the air with vaporous fears of intestine strifes and disgraceful misrule if England's protection (?) in minutest detail should be removed.

What course, then, does the Government pursue? Just what all falling despotisms in government compel: It assumes the names and forms of constitutional government; its " Irish members " sit in the House of Commons, but are powerless to secure legislation in the interest of their own constituents; it claims to administer justice according to English law, but its courts in Ireland exercise judicial functions under special acts of Parliament against which Englishmen would have rebelled. Meanwhile, the people of England, in the exercise of new powers and by attrition with democracies elsewhere, demand more for themselves and are keener to see the rightfulness of Ireland's claim and to recognize her cause as kindred to their own. English Liberals and Irish Parnelites, under the great statesman Gladstone, will ultimately secure not only Home Rule for Ireland, but a triumphant democracy wherever the British flag floats.

CHAPTER VI.

INDUSTRIAL DESPOTISM.

WHAT shall we eat, what shall we drink and wherewithal shall we be clothed? is a universal question; the character of the answer given is the test of the civilization of any age or country. Ireland's desolation appears in the answer which she gives. Potatoes, whiskey, rags; these are the ensign of her woe. An intelligent co-operation with Providence, in soil, climate and natural resource, guarantees the necessary provision for human needs. The ignorant or spiritless co-operation by the Irish people, the forcible repression or prohibition of co-operation by the British Government, these causes, singly or in unison, have thwarted the benign designs of the "Heavenly Father, who knoweth that his children have need of these things."

That we may the better understand England's industrial and commercial legislation concerning Ireland, and know the causes which directly or indirectly operated to almost wholly extinguish the industries of Ireland, we will divide the last four hundred years into four periods, these being marked by distinctive legislative policies. Credulity will be taxed in receiving the attested facts of history, and philanthropy will be pained at their illustration of "man's inhumanity to man" underneath this cloak of so-called commercial legislation.

First Period — Industrial Growth. From Poyning's Law, 1495, to Amended Navigation Act, 1663.

Second Period — Industrial Decay and Death. From 1663 to the Independent Irish Parliament, known as Grattan's Parliament, 1782.

Third Period — Industrial Resurrection. From 1782 to the Union, 1800.

Fourth Period — Industrial Decline. From 1800 to the present time.

First period — 1495 to 1663. During this period English and Irish industries grew side by side, both stimulated by natural resources and growing demands, and both

Industrial Despotism. 75

equally protected from the free imports of other nations. Her chief industries were woollen (fustian, flannels, broadcloths), linen, silk, hemp, sugar, hides and leather, soap, candles and salt. Cattle, sheep and horses were largely exported. In this even-handed industrial race Ireland well held her own, and threatened to seriously compete with the wealth and commercial enterprise of England.

Second Period — 1663 to 1782. In the amended Navigation Act of 1663 Ireland was left out. Lord North said of it: " The first commercial restriction was laid on Ireland not directly, but by a side wind and by deductive interpretation." The prohibitions of this act were not, however, left to " deductive interpretation." The act prohibited all exports from Ireland to the colonies, and the importation of Irish cattle into England. Subsequently an act declared such importation to be "a publick and common nuisance." In 1670 all importation to Ireland from the English plantations of sugar, tobacco, cotton-wool, indigo, ginger, fustic or other native dyeing wood was prohibited.

The energy driven back from trade sought exercise in cultivation of manufactures. Forbidden to export live cattle into England, they were killed and sent over as salted meats. An Act of Parliament soon prohibited this. The hides of the animals being still free, these were exported until — still suspicious and watchful — British dealers complained, and these were headed back to the hills where they were grown. Irish ingenuity, still contending for an outlet, worked up the hides into leather and thus bade fair to outwit the cupidity of English trade. Alas! Parliament relentlessly prohibited the exportation of leather! This procession of prohibitions, sounding the trumpet of English commercial despotism, loses even the pomp of power and assumes the fretful snarl of conscious decrepitude when we learn that candles were also under the ban of this rivalry, and not an Irish "tallow glim" could find its way across the channel. The woollen and linen industries, because of their natural pre-emption and early establishment, were soon the objects of jealous assault, first in the form of disabilities and later in actual prohibitions. It was unblushingly declared that this legislation was demanded because England's woollen manufactures suffered. There seems to have been no sense of moral obligation in the trade conscience of that era, and by an act of William III the woollen industry of Ireland was extinguished, and twenty thousand manufacturers left the island.

In this high-handed extinction of Ireland's natural and most productive manufacture, there was promised, in mitigation of damage, an advantage to the linen industry. Scotch Protestants were invited to Ireland under the specious plea that they should be afforded every possible assistance, and that Irish linen should be protected in the exclusive supply of the British market. Lord North says of this compact, "it was no sooner made than it was violated by England, for, instead of prohibiting foreign linens, duties were laid and collected, so far from amounting to a prohibition on the import of the Dutch, German and east country linen manufactures that those manufactures have been able, after having the duties imposed on them by the British Parliament, to undersell Ireland in Great Britain and the West Indies." Thus it was that Ireland's industries were pursued with relentless pertinacity, until the most searching scrutiny fails to discover a single one which was not fettered or prohibited by British Parliamentary acts, and this hostile legislation not only affected her relations with England, but with the commerce of the world. The flag of Ireland might wave in holiday splendor over the castles of her conquered princes, but was declared a commercial alien on the high seas.

The reader of Irish history during this period will learn that Ireland had then her own Parliament, and he may inquire why, then, did she hang as a suitor on English legislation; why did she not herself protect her own industries? why did she not go farther and meet England's aggressions with retaliatory measures? Simply because she could not. Her legislature, though a Parliament in name, had little representative character or executive power.

It was composed largely of Protestant

Industrial Despotism. 79

landlords. Political disabilities imposed by England, excluded the masses from representation, and even if it had been otherwise and the undivided voice of Parliament had sought industrial protection through Parliamentary acts, these acts would have been vetoed by the British Parliament or the Privy Council. "Poyning's Act," by which the Irish Parliament exercised its mock functions, expressly declared that no act should be adopted without the approval of the King of England or his Privy Council.

In the year 1771 the heads of a bill were introduced " to prevent corn from being made into whiskey and to put some restraint on the vice of drunkenness," which was increasing. The Lord Lieutenant of the day said " the whiskey shops were ruining the peasantry and the workmen. There was an earnest and general desire to limit them." " The Whiskey bill," says Mr. Froude, " was rejected because the Treasury (British) could not spare a few thousand pounds which were levied upon drunkenness." Thus poor Ireland, drunk to the health of the British revenue, garroted by Poyning's

Act, robbed by Birmingham and Manchester, was in as deplorable a condition as the "certain man" who journeyed from Jerusalem to Jericho. Thank God! the Good Samaritan from Hawarden Castle is passing by.

Third Period — 1782 to 1800. An Independent Parliament had long been the desire of Irish patriots. Henry Grattan was, more than any other, the champion of this new creation; it bears his name. Ireland at once opened her own ports to such of her manufactures as still survived. She felt through her whole commercial being the inspiration of a new life; but she did not at once turn upon England with retaliatory legislation. She waited to receive proffers of reciprocal intercourse. England was slow and surly, and at last yielded grudgingly some slight compromises. Then it was that Ireland, finally aroused, commenced legitimate retaliation. The marvelous growth of her manufactures and trade justified the dream of her patriots and the fear of her enemies. Secretary Foster said in 1785, three years after the liberation of Irish industries, "Britain imports annually two million five hundred thousand pounds of our products, all, or nearly all, duty free, and we import a million of hers, and raise a revenue on almost every article of it." In 1799, according to Mr. Pitt, "the imports from Great Britain were about the same, but the exports from Ireland to Britain had swelled to nearly six millions." Lord Clare, who was not very friendly to the Irish people, said, "There is not a nation on the face of the habitable globe which had advanced in cultivation, in manufactures, with the same rapidity in the same period — legislative independence — as Ireland."

Is it any wonder that the people of this country sit in the midst of their wrecked industries, behold their dilapidated factories, their silent mills, and bless the name of Gladstone and Home Rule, even as they revere the memory of Grattan and the days of legislative independence?

Fourth Period — 1800 to the present. The Legislative union of Great Britain and Ireland was effected in the year 1800. Lecky says of it: "It is a simple and unexaggerated statement of the fact that in the entire history of representative government there is no instance of corruption having been applied on so large a scale and with such audacious effrontery."

Mr. John Foster, the Speaker of the Irish House of Commons, in opposing the articles of union which set forth the commercial relations of the two countries, said: " They lower all protecting duties and expose the infant manufactures of Ireland (which the Irish Parliament had begun to protect) to the overwhelming competition of the great capital and long-established skill and ability of England. No less than seventy articles of our manufacture would be thus injured, and our cotton manufactures in particular, in which we had begun to make most promising advances, would be nearly ruined." This prophecy was fulfilled. Excepting only the linen trade of the North and a few scattered woollen mills, there are no industries in Ireland.

The policy long ago announced by Lord Stafford has found ample operation under the Union. "I am of opinion," said that lord, writing from Ireland to Charles I in 1634, "that all wisdom advises to keep this kingdom as much subordinate and dependent upon England as is possible, and holding them from the manufacture of wool, and then enforcing them to fetch their clothing from thence, and to take their salt from the king (being that which preserves and gives value to all their native staple commodities), how can they depart from us without nakedness and beggary?"

From the mass of England's tyrannies toward Ireland it is somewhat difficult to distinguish those which are purely economic, those which relate to racial and religious intolerance, and such as are overt and aggressive acts of political despotism. The pall of oppression is woven of many threads; the chain of bondage is welded of many links. Neither of these could alone have crushed this country; each was a bulwark of the other. Religious persecution could not have existed if through equal religious toleration those of the Catholic faith had been allowed to sit in the British Parliament. Neither could England have enforced trade and commercial servitude among the Irish people if they had at that time been under Home Rule. These conditions of political despotism and religious persecution so educated English thought and debauched the English conscience that it was no shock to her sense of justice to rob Ireland of her trade and commerce. It was easy to make of the political serf and the excommunicated heretic a beggar also. This England did. "He that breaketh one commandment is guilty of them all."

That these economic relations may be clearly understood, let us draw an illustration from current American economic life.

The energetic industrial life of the new South finds illustration in Georgia cotton manufactories and Alabama iron works. These already assume proportions which prophesy they will soon be entered in the competitive race with Massachusetts and Pennsylvania. Every well wisher of his country rejoices that, by this enlarged source of supplies, material advantage must come to the American consumer. The heart of the patriot is cheered in the contemplation

Industrial Despotism. 85

and present realization of the fact that trade and commerce, in their manifold ramifications, shall more closely unite the North and South in social and religious life, and educaional and philanthropic endeavor.

But suppose the government at Washington had the disposition and the power, at this time, to exclude Georgia and Alabama from the benefits of such reciprocal commercial relations with foreign powers as are secured by treaties; suppose these two States, by the very promise of their success, were marked as targets of industrial assault, and that they, without the power to protect by duties their own manufactures, were obliged to compete with the protected and bountied industries of Massachusetts and Pennsylvania; and suppose the Congress of the United States — adding insult to injury — should prohibit any exportation of cotton or iron from those States! The pen wearies, the tongue tires in giving expression to such an hypothesis! And yet such a course of injustice, robbery and industrial slaughter would be but the type of what England has done with Ireland.

Let it be remembered when studying the hypothetical and the historical results of "free trade" and "protection" that English industries were planted, nurtured and well established under a protective tariff, and even bounties, before the adoption of the present free trade policy.

Is there any sequence, or is it mere coincidence, that England's free trade policy was not adopted until Irish industries were destroyed and Irish nationality was well-nigh crushed; and Ireland's population of from five to eight millions, afforded an enforced, but ready, continual and convenient market for the manufactures of Manchester, Birmingham and Leeds? The cities of Belfast, Dublin and Cork were no longer shipping places for Irish exports, but were ports of entry and storehouses of English goods for Irish consumers. Is it inquired how could poverty-stricken Ireland afford any considerable market for manufactures of any kind? Let it be remembered that Ireland, though in herself poor, has received for years a steady income of millions of dollars every year from America. A high English authority estimates that up to a recent date this sum was equal to ten million dollars per annum. Much of this vast sum has been contributed by Irish servant-girls in the kitchens and nurseries of New York, Boston and Philadelphia, and by factory and mill operatives among the protected industries of New England and Pennsylvania. These Irish-Americans, often living in comparative comfort themselves, have been able through the Irish tenant and the Irish consumer thus to feed the greed of those twin despotisms, landlord absenteeism and commercial piracy.

Landlordism is doomed. A wholesale land purchase bill is one of Mr. Gladstone's beneficent measures for Ireland. Before many years these little tenant holdings shall have passed in fee simple to the actual tillers of the soil.

There is every promise that when Ireland shall have regained her local government she will again seek to nurture her industries, give employment to her people, and thus relieve the unnatural demand upon agriculture, which is one cause of the present agrarian troubles. Relieved from the political oppression of Dublin Castle Rule and the eighty-seven coercion acts of this century, her police barracks can easily be changed into warehouses, her whiskey shops to bakeries and her poorhouses to cattle sheds.

Then shall Ireland's answer to the universal question be more worthy the civilization of the on-coming twentieth century.

CHAPTER VII.

COERCION.

THE earliest records of all peoples touch disputes concerning land. First, (1) The individual wresting from his fellow a coveted hill or valley, then the tribe dispossessing by force their neighboring tribe; finally, on a larger and more extended scale, opposing nations came into conflict.

As a rule, the direct and principal object of all invasions, is to get possession of the land of the conquered country; this was true of the Jews, Vandals, Goths and Huns, and later of the Saxons, Danes and Normans.

By the natural laws of assimilation the conquered and the conqueror speedily fuse, and adopt similar laws, language and dress; Ireland was no exception to the operation of this law, and the original invaders readily assimilated to the Irish, and adopted their customs, manners and dress. This was too much for proud England, for did not all history teach that the weaker and conquered people speedily fused and adopted the customs and laws of their conquerors. The English people had fused with the Normans and had seen some of their cherished institutions swallowed up by the feudal system of the invaders; should the process be reversed by the low Irish peasant? No; not if England could prevent it.

Now begins the long and dreary series of Irish Coercion Acts. The first were aimed at the English colonists in Ireland, who were degenerating into "mere Irish" and would soon be absorbed by the "Irish enemy." This would be disastrous to English authority; hence the Kilkenny Statute, by which it was made high treason for the colonists to marry, bring up, foster, or stand sponsor to, any of the Irish, while any Englishman using an Irish name, wearing an Irish dress, speaking the Irish language, following the Irish custom of growing a moustache, or of riding without a saddle, had all of his possessions sold in atonement, or if a poor man, was condemned to imprisonment for life.

The folly of such petty and unjust acts of coercion is only equalled by its wickedness. The logic of events soon demonstrated that these impositions of unusual restraint on the liberty of innocent customs and habits were a complete failure, and many of the colonists became " More Irish than the Irish themselves."

The obvious injustice, and the failure of these first coercive measures taught England no lesson. Failing to prevent the growing moustache, the bare-back riding, and the operation of God's universal law of love, marriage and offspring, she found herself in danger of losing by absorption what little power Ireland already possessed, and, with hardness of heart, determined to try other coercive measures. Poyning's law was directed against Irish Nationality and provided that henceforth no Parliament should be held in Ireland "until the Chief-Governor had certified to the King under the Great Seal, as well the causes and considerations, as the Acts they desired to pass, and till the same should be approved by the King and Council." Thus were the Irish compelled to nullify their authority, and their Parliament became a farce.

These laws did not increase the love between the two peoples, nor were they calculated to make either natives or settlers law-abiding people. This exceptional interference by England in purely Irish affairs was conspicuously unjust and contrary to her uniform conduct with her other colonies, and the result proved that while England by coercion could manacle the Irish Parliament, she could not thereby compel loyal obedience to laws practically enacted at Westminster.

It is often claimed that religious differences are the chief causes of trouble between England and Ireland, but these instances of coercion occurred long before the Reformation, and when both islands professed the same creed, but so great was the mutual hatred in Ireland that Englishmen and Irishmen each built and worshiped in their own churches as exclusively as though some great difference of faith kept them apart.

In the progress of time the Reformation

Coercion. 93

swept over England, and she became Protestant. Of course the Irish people must be Protestant too. This was a sacred duty, and must be accepted as of right. They were to change their faith at the word of command. No attempt was made to convert them; the Bible was not even translated into Irish. The English Church service was to be read in English or Latin, by these merciless enemies, to a people who understood neither.

The result of this experiment failed. The Irish people were not to be converted in that way. Thus a new cause for coercive measures arose, and England was not slow to use it in vindicating the supremacy of her religion. All former oppression faded into insignificance before the stern "Penal Code" which was framed especially to coerce Papists into Protestants. The English Parliament at Westminster, and the more English Parliament in Ireland concurred in stripping the Catholics (comprising five sixths of the Irish people) of every vestige of civil, political and religious freedom.

The English historian Froude (who cannot be suspected of partiality to the Irish) has said: "The English government had added largely to their difficulty by attempting to force the Reformation on Ireland while its political and social condition was still unsettled. The Irish were not to be blamed if they looked to the Pope, to Spain, to France, to any friend in earth or heaven to deliver them from a power that discharged no single duty that rulers owe to subjects."

What was effected by these coercive laws? Priests were driven from their flocks, bishops and prelates put to death, church property was confiscated, and open mass gagged. The Reformation had come with crushing ferocity, and the "supremacy of England's ecclesiastical laws was vindicated."

But what of the Irish spirit and the Catholic faith? Were these crushed? No indeed. The very brutalities of which the coercionists of that period were guilty, did but serve to intensify their faith in and love for Romanism.

The tangible Romish Church in Ireland

Coercion. 95

was for the time suppressed, but England forgot that the intangible, the ideal, the sentimental are just as real, and must be considered; that faith and love are facts as actual as powder and shot. The Irish clung to their faith, the English to their guns, and the fact that Romanism is stronger in Ireland to-day than in any other nation on the face of the globe outside of the distinctively papal countries of Europe and South America, ought to teach the English government that the Armstrong gun will not crush out Irish nationalism, but will intensify it.

Thus centuries of coercive measures failed to destroy Irish character, Irish customs or Irish faith.

But proud England would not be baffled, and what she failed to do by force, she now seeks to do by fraud and stratagem.

It is at least a change to turn our attention from coercion to seduction. England now commenced to draw Ireland into the "union" by the influences of promises of titles, of political preferment, and a "judicious expenditure" of over ten millions of dollars among the members of the Irish

Parliament, all Protestants, and accomplished the tangible fact of "union." The articles were agreed to by the two Parliaments, and the rewards were duly bestowed on the violent abductors of the Irish Parliament.

The Irish people are informed that they are united with England, and dragged reluctant and protesting to the bridal chamber. Was the sentiment of the Irish people changed? No; except to make them detest England all the more.

How absurd to apply the name of "union," which means concord, to a condition which is the result of seduction, abduction and coercion. What concord has existed between the two peoples during the eighty-seven years that have elapsed since the consummation of this unnatural crime?

In twenty-two of the first thirty years of the so-called "union" the Habeas Corpus Act was suspended and eighteen Coercive Acts, or acts of a similar nature, passed. This fraudulent union has brought Ireland in eighty-seven years, eighty-seven coercion acts. The last and the most severe of all is aimed to crush the Irish National League which the Irish people believe is "their salvation," and which alone stands between them and the most cruel oppression. And this is done with the deliberate and avowed object of destroying the political organization of the Irish people.

On the twenty-fourth day of September, in the year of our Lord 1887, a decision is made according to the law and the testimony which presents to the world in ugly hieroglyphics, England's version of constitutional liberty in Ireland under the last Coercion Act.

The arrest, under the Crimes Bill, of William O'Brien,* for an alleged violation of the right of free speech, the denial to him of trial by a jury, his conviction and sentence to three months' imprisonment by two stipendiary magistrates of Dublin Castle, this is an heroic page in the history of Ireland's march for constitutional liberty.

The circumstances of the case were that, on the ninth and eleventh of August, 1887,

* My apology for giving so full an account of the trial of William O'Brien lies in the hope that it will serve to illustrate the methods used by England in enforcing coercion laws. I was present and witnessed the trial. The accompanying details are taken almost verbatim from an account written at the time.

William O'Brien, a member of the British Parliament, addressed his constituents at Mitchelstown, County of Cork, Ireland, on general political issues. Among other things he advised tenants concerning the manner in which they should meet the processes of eviction then pending. He set forth the Plan of Campaign as the wisest course by which to maintain their holdings until the new act of Parliament, giving the tenants greater reduction in rent than many of them had dared to ask and which was soon to go into operation, would give redress. In the meanwhile they were advised to "defend their homes by all honest means, and to make evictions as slow and as expensive to the Government as possible."

His advice was followed, and not another eviction was successfully carried out. The five hundred tenants on the Mitchelstown estate can now go into the Land Court and claim the provisions of the new law.

The Crimes Bill, under which Mr. O'Brien was arrested, provides for the arrest and trial by summary proceeding before two resident magistrates and without jury " of any person who shall incite any other person to resist a minister of the law in the execution of his duty." The trial was conducted in the court house, and seemed more like a military than a civil proceeding. The prisoner entered town in an open carriage, preceded by Scotch fusileers, surrounded by armed constabulary and mounted hussars. A procession of open carriages bringing brother members of Parliament — Irish and English — and other friends and representatives of Irish nationalism followed the prisoner. At the court house ladies presented flowers and displayed the ribbon of green.

The military and constabulary were variously disposed in the court room, about the entrance, in the square opposite and across the common highway on either side the main entrance to the town. Neighing horses, nodding plumes, glittering steel, brilliant red coats, armed men drawn up before the entrance to a court house, and all for what? Why is all this display, this show of war? Has Russia marched on Bulgaria, have Bismarck and Von Moltke broken the Triple Alliance, has Napoleon's ghost arisen and has Wellington called to arms? O no! This is only William O'Brien — the man who could not be hired to run away — and the unarmed peasants who have come to do him honor. The court consisted of two resident magistrates appointed by Dublin Castle. They represented in physique and general bearing typical English gentlemen.

William O'Brien, the prisoner at the bar, was the centre of interest — a tall, spare man, with large features, a strongly marked intellectual development, piercing eyes even through the glasses which he always wears, quick, almost nervous in movement and intense in nature and convictions. He looked a little worn from confinement and his journey hither; he neither smiled nor frowned at the testimony of witness, the sparring of counsel or the rulings of the court. Confronted with representatives of the Crown, really partisans of a Tory Government which he had defied, surrounded by military and armed constabulary, from whom his accusers are taken, as one after another testified against him he was as calm and self-poised as if in his editorial chair at Dublin. The room was densely packed and all were friends save the officers of the Crown and their servants. His counsel, Mr. T. Harrington M. P., and Mr. Mandeville of Mitchelstown, were personal friends and brother-patriots as well. They conducted a vigorous and powerful defence.

Next in interest, but not second in the affections of the people, is John Dillon, who sits close by intently watching the proceedings. Now and then slowly rising with simple dignity, his calm eyes quietly assure the eager throng that, however this case may go, the battle brings final victory to Ireland. There emanates from this strong, quiet man, who seldom smiles, an irresistible moral power; it compels the respectful consideration of his enemies, it inspires confidence and cements devotion among his followers. This is true in a limited sense of a dozen or more lesser leaders whom the people trust and obey.

These leaders have been more effective as a self-constituted police among these surging multitudes than the Castle constabulary or Her Majesty's Hussars. The organizer and commander of this voluntary local police is John Mandeville, brother to Mr. O'Brien's counsellor, himself under arrest for the same so-called incendiarism. From his prison cell he districted the town and stationed his men; in citizens' clothes and without arms, they have kept the peace, notwithstanding the people were annoyed with the show and interference of military authority, and aggravated at the spectacle of their heroic defender in Parliament and at home, on trial for the strong, helpful words he had uttered to and for them. What a spectacle! A member of Parliament on trial as a disturber of the peace, an inciter to incendiarism, his co-defendant in jail awaiting trial for a similar offence; these two alleged criminals holding in check thousands of men impassioned by poverty and sense of outrage, but who for this repressive moral power might have thrown themselves across this last dead line of England's nineteenth century coercion policy!

The heroic and the pathetic are strangely blended in this passing history. A few brave men, with love of God, of country and of human rights, make their protest against the hoary legal intrenchments of landed aristocracies. With self-abnegation they labor without ceasing, they endure all things, they risk all things. This is heroism. The unquestioning loyalty of poor, ignorant men, the tender, almost worshipful devotion of women and little children, the benediction of the aged, these are pathetic. Very touching are some manifestations of these people. Among the multitudes who crowded about the door as O'Brien entered the court was a decrepit old woman, who gazed reverently as the adored hero passed. With hands clasped in attitude of prayer she said: " Indeed I'm praying His holy name, and the blessed Mary and Joseph and all the rest of thim, that there'll no harm come to any one to-day. Sure and might not we be patient; did not Himself suffer more than any of us, and His blessed mother looking at Him all the time?"

While the crowd cheered and threw their caps in air at sight of their heroes, along its fringe were many tearful women who feebly swayed with weight of anguished years, which left in them no power to utter sound. As dies the last tone of a muffled bell, when the funeral train has passed, so they looked silent on. When Ireland's coming day shall have arisen from this red morn these mourners will be resting underneath the verdant sod, but their children and their children's children shall be free.

Mr. T. Harrington, the leading counsel for Mr. O'Brien, is a typical Irishman, impetuous to ferocity, humorous to hilarity, at times incisive and cold as steel, and again hot as burning lava. He follows the witness on cross-examination with the seeming recklessness of a trained acrobat or the merciless grip of a professional pugilist. The case for the Crown rested on the testimony of three policemen, who took the stand, armed and in full uniform. It is the custom for the Government on its own behalf to detail a reporter for popular Irish gatherings, that an official account of the meetings and the very words of the speakers may be known to the Castle. Much annoyance and doubtless some intimidation has been occasioned by this custom. During the progress of the

case on behalf of the Crown, and after the
introduction of several witnesses, whose testimony failed to sustain the charge, the
Crown rested without calling Constable
O'Sullivan, who was the official reporter of
the meeting at which O'Brien spoke. Then
occurred a dramatic scene, the like of which
is seldom witnessed in a court room. Mr.
Harrington sprang to his feet and exclaimed,
"Is it possible, Your Worships, that the Crown
will close this case without calling Head
Constable O'Sullivan, who was that day in
charge of the peace of the town, and who
certainly should be able to give material testimony?" To this the Crown counsel coolly
replied: "The case for the Crown has
closed," repeating the answer several times
in response to Mr. Harrington's exclama-
tions of surprise. "Very well, then," said
Harrington, "I ask Your Worship for a
summons for Head Constable O'Sullivan."
After some words as to the cowardice of the
Crown in not producing its own officer as a
witness, and the taunting retort that if this
witness were called by the defence they must
be bound by his testimony, Mr. Harrington

said: "Very well, then, I take him as my witness, hostile though he certainly will be." After the confusion attending this seeming recklessness had subsided, O'Sullivan appeared and was sworn.

Following preliminary questions as to his being in charge of the force on that day, his presence at the meeting, his taking notes of Mr. O'Brien's speech, Counsel Harrington asked him to produce the notes. He answered he would not unless directed by his superior officer. The Court was evidently inclined to shield the witness, and seemed confused as to a conflict of authority between himself and the Royal Constabulary, to which the witness was subordinate. After some consultation the officer in command, with sword dangling from his belt, stepped to the witness, and, after conference, permitted him to produce the notes. They were fuller and more carefully prepared than those of previous witnesses; they were far less objectionable in tenor and actual signification; indeed, a case against Mr. O'Brien could not have been sustained by that report of his speech. It was then quite evident why the Crown had not produced this witness. Faces before listless became intense, and interest deepened to indignation when, on examination by counsel, it was discovered that the resistance advocated by Mr. O'Brien was qualified by the noble adjective "honest." This word was omitted from the notes of former witnesses of the Crown, and when it was further discovered that upon the margin of the paper on which the notes were written was penciled in another hand, "not to be used," and that this official report had been carried by the witness to Dublin Castle; that a conference with the Crown counsel and the Divisional Inspector of Royal Constabulary — Capt. Plunkett by name — had there been held; that one of the here presiding judges on that very day, and from that very place, had issued the summons for the arrest of Mr. O'Brien; when one after another these circumstances of a manifest conspiracy by civil and military officers of the Crown to jeopardize the liberty of a citizen by suppressing exculpatory testimony in its possession; when with cumulative force this all appeared, it is not strange that a powerful impression was evident in that

crowded court room. Counsel for the Crown
was dumb, the witness crimsoned, the impli-
cated judge attempted a personal defence.
Counsel Harrington, rising to his utmost
height, seized the unpretending paper, and,
with terrible force, denounced the whole proceedings as a mockery of justice and a disgrace to the Empire. Gathering up his papers
and brief, he said: " I will not further disgrace
myself by practicing before this court." Meanwhile, the most unmoved of all the throng
were the prisoner at the bar and his friend,
John Dillon. In the midst of the excite-
ment the Court adjourned. The Court, at
the opening of the next day's sessions, com-
mented on the unfortunate occurrence of the
preceding day, and severely reprimanded Mr.
Harrington — he, however, was absent — and
stated that the dignity of the Court must be
sustained. To this Mr. O'Brien (now acting
without counsel) replied. He fully justified
Mr. Harrington's general conduct of the case
and his course in the circumstances under
criticism; he expressed high appreciation of
the distinguished ability and legal acumen
displayed in wresting from a prejudiced court

Coercion.   109

and an intriguing counsel evidence of a
Dublin Castle plot to suppress official testimony, and thus endanger his liberty and perhaps his life. While he thus justified his
devoted friend, he found himself deprived of
his valuable service, and must conduct his
further defence alone. In impassioned majesty, and self-conscious integrity, his illumined face bore no trace of despair.

"Ulysses stood alone, but stood collected
in himself and whole." Mr. O'Brien closed
in his own defence. He declared the construction of the Court unconstitutional, the
judges biased by subordination to political
and military authority, the Crown counsel
manifestly guilty of prejudicing his cause by
a suppression of official testimony, and he
denounced the ostentatious display of constabulary and military force as an insult to
the Irish people, whose representative he was.
He claimed that the Crown had utterly failed
to establish a case against him, but disclaimed
any desire to deny or apologize for or weaken
any advice he had given or any words he
had spoken. He rejoiced that his advice had
been so generally followed, and that so many

poor tenants, by it, had been saved from utter ruin. He reviewed the deplorable condition of the people, their sense of outrage at the course pursued by the land agents, and boldly declared that, far from being a disturber of the peace and an inciter to lawlessness, he was a conservator of the peace and a friend of good government. He appealed from this court to the Irish people, to the English Democracy, and to the civilized world. While listening to his wonderful plea, one forgot that he was the prisoner at the bar, and thought of him as a chief amid his clan, a hero of heroes, a seer among statesmen, a Christian patriot ready to live and labor or suffer and die for his country. Of what consequence to him then was the three months' sentence that the Mitchelstown Court imposed upon him? 'Tis but a speck of time; a comma in the record of his life's work. In the long perspective of history he shall stand among heroes. In the heap of manacles, and whips, and chains, and tortuous engines of earth's tyrannies shall be seen the bands he broke, the fetters he unloosed. Multitudes of Ireland's poor shall call him blessed.

CHAPTER VIII.

THE IRISH LAND QUESTION.

IN tracing England's dealings with Ireland in the matters of government, religion and commerce, we have pointed out how these were affected by the land question. It is the one question which has been in dispute during the whole period since the conquest, and which still lies at the root of Ireland's difficulties.

Seven hundred years of strife and tumult, of injustice and violence, have passed away, and still the conflict goes on.

That we may the better comprehend the agrarian wrongs which the people now suffer, and the nature and scope of the recent land acts passed, it is well to examine the causes of this perpetual conflict.

As already shown, conquest, confiscation and coercion were the means used by the English to acquire possession of lands in Ireland.

If the proportion of the English colonists in Ireland had approached in number that of the native Irish population, and if they had maintained actual possession of these stolen lands, a complete organization of society on the English system of Land Tenure might have been the result, and the strife might have ended. But such was not the case; the best land was taken by force and parcelled out to colonists, or allotted to noblemen who lived in England, the native Irish being driven on to the poorer lands. The real estate of the English colonist was held under the Feudal System.

By the thirteenth century the custom of Primogeniture had become absolute in England. By this law the eldest son had the exclusive right to succeed to his father's estates. The Irish had quite another system of Land Tenure; the land was divided between different clans and families on an equitable basis, and when a member of a sept or clan died, the chief divided the lands afresh among the remaining members, the heirs of the deceased receiving, share and share, alike. This was the Common Law of the country ; the immemorial usage handed down through long generations.

It is evident that this conflict in tenure might open the door to countless disputes; and this was the fact.

This point is one which it is necessary to dwell upon, because it will help to explain many of the anomalies of the Land question.

During the two centuries that followed the invasion of Ireland by Henry II the Tribal System of Tenure prevailed over the greater part of the Island. Many of the English barons had left their estates and returned to England; indeed, many had never taken actual and visible possession of their Irish lands; these estates were repossessed by the Irish people, and again came under tribal laws and customs, while the members of septs and clans again became co-proprietors, and retained possession for many generations.

Thus we see engrafted on the same land and at the same time the two systems of tenures ; the paper title in the absent Englishman from the Crown, representing the

Feudal System, and the tribal title, with actual possession, granted by the chief representing the Tribal System.

In the progress of time these lands became more valuable and the English owners or their heirs at law began to look them up and claim their rights; this brought on a conflict between the invaded and the invaders; a conflict of two systems. Thus was inaugurated a struggle between two peoples which has never ceased, and never will, until it is possible for the Irishman to become the owner of the soil of his country on an equitable basis.

We have briefly summarized the land tenures of Ireland, from Henry II to Charles II — nearly five centuries; and this was the time it took to destroy the Tribal System, though as a matter of fact it was not entirely replaced by the English System; for while the English landlord reaped the benefits of the Feudal System of tenure, he used the old Sept System when it could be applied to the prejudice of the tenant. The landlord as chief of the sept, had forcibly taken all its land; and the Irish tenants, the members of the sept, paid rent to this chief, and made all improvements at their own expense.

This dual system of land tenure is a fruitful cause of Ireland's griefs, and will prepare the mind of the reader to appreciate the difficulties which beset the English Parliament in attempting now after centuries of these oppressive systems, to adjust the relations of landlord and tenant.

In 1870 the First Land Act became law and the English people doubtless believed that at last Ireland's wrong had been righted.

The debates in Parliament at that time show that the pleas of the more advanced Irish party were not listened to; they persistently claimed that the act did not go to the root of the disease, and that in some respects it would aggravate the evil.

The act sought to create fixity of tenure for the tenant, so long as he should pay his rent, and to insure him compensation for the improvements which he had made. It was an imperfect measure, and the views of the Irish members were soon shown to be correct. The landlords had retained " their power to arbitrarily increase their rents, irrespective of the value of the holdings of their estates." The act only provided for compensation for improvements in case of arbitrary eviction; when a tenant was evicted for non-payment of rent he lost his right. If for any cause a landlord desired to evict a tenant, and retain the improvements without compensation, it was an easy matter to make the rent sufficiently high to accomplish the object. In some instances rents were raised as high as five hundred per cent.

In the three years before this Land Act was passed there were served four thousand two hundred and fifty-three notices to quit; in the three years after, five thousand six hundred and forty-one, and in seven years after they had doubled. This first act failed " to diffuse the blessings of peace, order and industry, over a smiling land" as was prophesied. Why did it fail? Because Englishmen would not take the advice of the Irish leaders, but persisted in looking at questions purely Irish through English spectacles.

Between 1871 and 1880 no less than twenty-eight measures to amend or extend the provisions of this Land Act of 1870 were introduced into Parliament, but not one of them was carried.

The Irish people, despairing of obtaining justice from agitation in the English Parliament, were again forced into the adoption of means which were contrary to law and order, and terrible outrages were committed, which were deplored by none more than by the Irish leaders themselves. These outrages caused new coercive acts to be passed, and poor Ireland was again in an alarmingly disturbed state. The landlords organized, and fearing the growing sentiment in England in favor of a new land bill, that would compel compensation in all instances of eviction, they made the most of their time and opportunity, and writs of evictions came thick and fast upon the poor tenants.

What marvel then that, during this period of ten years, Irishmen should organize for self-protection? The Home Rule League and the Land League were organized for the purpose of uniting all creeds and opinions in favor of Home Rule and Land Reform for Ireland. These carried on a marvelous and world-wide agitation, and by united efforts in 1880 succeeded in increasing the number of their representatives in the English Parliament to sixty members.

The thought of the English people was again turned to Ireland. Beaconsfield announced his intention of appealing to the people, and officially denounced the Home Rule party. The Liberal Party, which was known to be in favor of remedial legislation for Ireland came into power at the general election of 1880, with Gladstone as their leader. The first act of the new Government was to appoint a Royal Commission to inquire into the working of the Land Act of 1870. It is interesting to read the report of that commission, and its recommendations, and to note how fully this report sustained the prophecy of the Irish leaders. It was to the effect that while the Land Bill had failed to produce any reform in the system of land tenure in Ireland, it had not checked unreasonable increase in rents, nor had it lessened evictions.

In 1881 Mr. Gladstone made an earnest and bold attempt to deal with the land question. A measure introduced by him was intended to secure fair rents, fair sale, and fixity of tenure. A principal feature was the creation of a Land Court, by which all disputes between landlord and tenant might be decided. A tenant going before this court could have his holding appraised, and the judicial rent thus fixed controlled for fifteen years; during this time no rise in rent was to be possible, and no eviction, save for nonpayment of rent, could take place. In case the tenant wished to sell the good-will of his holding, he could do so. This bill after being sent back by the House of Lords three times was finally agreed to, and passed on the twenty-second day of August, 1881.

What a strange fatuity! The chosen representatives of Ireland who took part in the debates on this bill have suffered imprisonment for agitating the very views which it formulated.

It will be noticed that this bill, creating a new land tenure, gave to the Irish tenant great privileges, and created what is practically known as a joint-ownership in the soil. It was an infringement of the rights of property, and presents one of the anomalies of this Irish Land Question. It deprived the landlord of fixing the value of his own property, and practically declared that part of the value of the land is the just possession of the tenant.

Again England's statesmen congratulated the country that the perplexing land question in Ireland was forever settled. But the events which had produced so great a change in public opinion in England, as to render it possible that such a bill could become law, had produced a corresponding advance in Irish demands, and the land bill which ten years before would have satisfied them, now received only their cold approval, and was accepted as merely a half-measure. And such it proved to be. Thousands rushed to the court to have a fair rent fixed; within the first two years over seventy-five thousand were fixed by the land court, sixty-six thousand by agreement between the landlord and the tenant, and over ten thousand by the county court; an average of all of these shows that the rents were reduced twenty per cent.

Surely no stronger case for the justice of the tenant's claim could be made out, for according to the scale of fair rent as fixed by the court he had for years been paying twenty per cent too much to the landlord.

Mr. Gladstone with the best intentions towards the Irish people, tried to settle the Land Question by this bill. He made a mighty effort to uproot this upas-tree of centuries' growth. He would have measurably succeeded but for the unusual depression of more than twenty per cent in agricultural products, since these fair rents were fixed, and but for the further fact that many of the tenants by reason of being unable to pay back rents, could not take the benefits of the act, while others had no money to expend in ordinary court expenses.

It will thus be seen that the landlords were still masters of the situation, and no one saw this sooner than did Mr. Gladstone himself. Again he addressed himself to the question of the remedy. To his mind the time had come to do full and complete justice to Ireland, according to the Irish idea, and to this end he introduced in 1885 the Home Rule and Land Purchase bills. These gave to Ireland an independent parliament with full power of dealing with all local matters including land; they reserved imperial guarantees for imperial matters, — such as the army, navy and finance, — and used the imperial credit as a means of transforming the tenure of land and of buying out landlords who were unwilling to remain under the new order of things.

This scheme, generous, wise and statesmanlike, is worthy of the great man who conceived it. With unmovable allegiance to justice, and with sublime faith in the future, he chose, when it was rejected, to retire from the office of Prime Minister of the British Empire, and to abide the verdict of the people.

CHAPTER IX.

THE UNION.

THE agitation for Home Rule for Ireland compels a recurrence to what some term ancient history, but as the Bishop of Westchester has well said, "The roots of the present lie deep in the past."

If the Irish people had voluntarily entered into the union with Great Britain, and if the conditions of the union had been fulfilled by both parties to the act — an act involving such vast interests, and affecting so many vested rights — it should have been regarded as sacred and binding until dissolved by mutual consent; but if, on the other hand, the Irish Parliament with the show of local government was wrested from the Irish people by fraud and violence and they were betrayed into the union, it matters a great deal, and mere lapse of time cannot bar the right to full restitution.

Previous to 1782 legislation in the Irish Parliament was controlled by the English Privy Council, through the provisions of the celebrated statute known as the Poyning's Law. In 1782 this statute was modified and the Irish Parliament was in theory independent, though practically it was largely controlled by English influence, as Catholics were still ineligible.

From 1782 to 1800 during the period of Parliamentary independence there was great increase in prosperity admitted by the foremost advocates " of the union," as shown in a previous chapter.

This brings us down to the time of the unholy Union and leads us to inquire into the methods used to accomplish it.

The debates on the Act of Union in the British Parliament show conclusively that Birmingham and Manchester feared the growing industries of Ireland as being disadvantageous to them ; indeed the contrivers of the union before 1799 avowed to each other "that the great object of their work was a stoppage of the growing prosperity of Ireland "; they probably did not

The Union. 125

dream of so complete an attainment of that end as has been achieved.

While touching upon the real motive of the English Government, we ought not to omit the evident intention, as it has finally resulted, of making the Irish people share in the English national debt; not on a pro rata basis by putting in the comparatively small Irish national debt (though this was at first proposed), but by making the otherwise oppressed and impoverished nation bear as much of the debt of both countries as could possibly be wrung from it.

In 1880 the Irish national debt was only twenty-one millions, whereas the English national debt was four hundred and forty-six millions, and the union was advocated on the ground that by this means Ireland would be subject to British taxes.

Mr. Posthlewait in writing about the desirability of the union said, " By the union Ireland would soon be enabled to pay a million a year toward the taxes of Great Britain beside the full support of their own establishment." Then comes this remarkable passage (which displays the desire of the shark to unite with its prey): "As England does already possess no inconsiderable share of the lands of Ireland, so the union would prove an effectual method to vest the rest in her; for as the riches of Ireland would chiefly return to England, she containing the seat of the empire, the few Irish landlords left would be little better than tenants to her for allowing them the privilege of making the best of their estates."

The fear of a French invasion was also a reason for the establishment of the union. "Had Napoleon taken his fleet to Ireland instead of to Egypt, the power of England might have been annihilated, and in after years Napoleon saw how fatal had been his error; but Pitt and the other English statesmen saw the danger at the time, and knowing the widespread disaffection in Ireland, they perceived as Napoleon did not, that, invaded by a French fleet the Ireland of 1798 might have become a French province to the inevitable ruin of the British empire."

This deep-seated fear (felt though not acknowledged) having taken possession of England's rulers it became an incentive for the most powerful efforts that could be put forth for national preservation, and a survey of the field developed all that diplomacy could devise, all that stratagem combined with military power, could accomplish, aided by bribery and intimidation.

With the general view of making the Act of Union more likely to pass, even though it might not be popular, the Act of Catholic Emancipation was discussed and virtually promised. This act had already become popular with the Irish people — Protestants as well as Catholics. Lord Fitzwilliam was appointed as Lord Lieutenant of Ireland. He was known to be favorable to such an act, and numerous petitions for its enactment were sent to him on his arrival in the country.

In February, 1795, Grattan brought in a bill which Sir William Pitt, then Prime Minister, approved; but the king announcing his opposition, Pitt was obliged to reverse his policy or resign his office; he preferred the former course; the Lord Lieutenant was recalled, his appointments reversed, and Grattan's bill was supported by a minority of only forty-eight. The cup of concession, held thus temptingly to the lips of Ireland, was dashed away by royal caprice; the people were exasperated, and the rebellion of 1798 soon made its dreadful record. Seventy thousand persons perished in this intermittent civil war if that may be called a civil war which is represented on one side by a powerful and rapacious army and on the other by a people enfeebled by poverty, weighed down by superstition, and only sustained by a sense of inalienable right, a love of home and fireside, the renown of their ancestry treasured in legendary ballad and historical record, and in such race inter-lineaments as assured them of their rightful heritage.

In order to veil a portion of the heinousness of this act, it was thought necessary to make it appear to be a measure popular with the people. Lord Cornwallis therefore travelled through a portion of the country obtaining signatures to a petition for the union; these he secured by persuasion, intimidation, dissimulation, and under or while martial law was in operation. He succeeded in obtaining about three thousand names, while the patriot party obtained about seven hundred and seven thousand signatures against the act. "Twenty-seven counties," says Mr. Sheridan, "declared against the union, and with these there would have been included, if martial law had not been proclaimed and prevented the intended meetings, the counties of Antrim and Sligo. If the measure was thus to be carried I have no hesitation in saying that it was an act of tyranny and oppression, and must become the fatal source of new discontents and future rebellions."

An ugly feature of this conspiracy of diplomacy and power was the subornation of the Independent Parliament of Ireland, known as Grattan's Parliament. At a time when the country had become comparatively prosperous through equitable laws administered by it in the interest of that country, this Parliament was virtually annulled by the suborning of a large majority of its members by British bribes and a terrorizing diplomacy.

The purchase of representative boroughs and the unseating of members not favorable to the union are well-authenticated facts which "he who runs may read." This latter move was effected by a technical perversion of the "Place Bill" and by substituting members to vote for the union, though against their every sense of right, and the proffer of English peerages.

Thus what all other means could not do was effected by bribery and political corruption. " Twenty-two Irish peerages," it is stated, " were created, five peers received English peerages, and twenty peers received higher titles."

When defending himself in the state trials before a jury composed exclusively of Unionists, Mr. O'Connell affirmed without fear of contradiction: " You know that there were one million two hundred and seventy-five thousand pounds actually spent in the purchase of rotten boroughs. You know that there were three million pounds besides expended in actual payment of the persons who voted for the union."

Mr. Lecky says: " The ministers, by money and dignities, had bought almost all the great nomination borough owners, as well as a large proportion of the members, and this made their success certain."

Each seat was valued at seven thousand five hundred pounds, and the whole sum awarded amounted to one million two hundred and sixty thousand pounds.

The proposition was at first defeated in the Irish Parliament by a vote of one hundred and nine to one hundred and four. Public enthusiasm ran high and the illumination of Dublin attested the feeling of the people:

Two days after the defeat of the measure in the Irish House of Commons Lord Cornwallis wrote a secret and confidential letter to the Duke of Cortland, in which he says:

"The late experiment has shown the impossibility of carrying the measure, which is contrary to the private interests of those who are to decide it, and which is not supported by the country at large."

The measure was carried, however, on June 7, 1800, and received the royal assent on August 2nd of the same year; "the prolonged struggle between the Patriot party and the British cabinet" was for the time concluded and "an independent kingdom began to be governed by alien officials in whose selection she had no voice; her National Parliament filled with nominees of these officials, and of the House of Lords."

The Act of Union became operative in 1801, and was in that year sustained by a standing army of one hundred and twenty-nine thousand two hundred and fifty-eight men; an increase from less than eight thousand, used to crush the rebellion of 1798, which was intended to express the popular will against the union.

This was an early fruit of the "peace and good will" promised to result from the union.

It is a well-acknowledged principle in the courts of the civilized world, that a contract which has been brought about by misrepresentation or fraud is not only voidable, but void *ab initio*, and that it is the duty of courts of equity to not only declare such contracts void, but, if possible, to place the parties in the same position as they were before the contract was entered into. When England returns to Ireland her "Home

The Union.   133

Rule," and makes such disposition of the Land Question as is just and equitable, she will then have but complied with the original rules of justice that are compelled between man and man.

If, however, the means used to carry the union had been lawful and right, and if the action of the Irish Parliament had been unbiased by fraud or intimidation, the question may still be asked, Where did that Parliament get its authority to annul the Irish constitution and to deliver the government to England?

The people of Ireland, as far as they had a voice, sent their delegates to Dublin to make laws under the constitution of Ireland and for that commonwealth, but instead of doing what they were elected to do, they arrogated to themselves the power to transfer their authority to the Parliament at Westminster. Lord Chancellor Plunkett denied the competency of the Irish Parliament to do this act in the most express terms. " I warn you," he said, " do not lay your hands on the constitution; I tell you that if, circumstanced as you are, you pass this act, it will be a mere nullity, and no man in Ireland will be bound to obey it; you have not been elected for that purpose; you were elected to make laws, and appointed to exercise the functions of legislators, not to transfer them; you are appointed to act under the constitution, not to destroy it."

This was sound doctrine, founded on the immutable laws of right and reason, but it did not prevail, and Ireland's constitution and government were taken by force.

Froude says: "If there be one lesson which history clearly teaches, it is this: that free nations cannot govern subject provinces. If they are unable or unwilling to admit their dependencies to share their own constitution, the constitution itself will fall in pieces from mere incompetence for its duties."

May it not be that the spirit of Anglican Liberty long outraged by England in her treatment of Ireland, is now an avenging angel fighting Ireland's cause; and that the forces thus working out her salvation, are the silent forces protecting the Englishman in his constitutional rights?

CHAPTER X.

HOME RULE.

GREAT epochs in the progress of constitutional liberty have been marked by popular agitation, by sanguinary strife, legislative controversy and judicial decisions. The Irish cause now attracting the attention of the world is marked by these distinguishing features. It is kin to Israel's revolt from Egyptian task-makers; its leaders are brother patriots of those of Sparta, Greece, Poland, Hungary, Switzerland. Its principles are justified by the Magna Charta and the Bill of Rights; by the American Declaration of Independence and the Emancipation Proclamation of Abraham Lincoln.

Why should it be thought a thing incredible that a people with clearly marked race and creed distinctions, with an individual history and a national spirit, and dwelling in a country separated from all others by tempestuous seas, should desire self-government? When it is remembered that Ireland is such a country and that for hundreds of years she was unconquered, while her neighbor England yielded to successive invasions, is it surprising that she now protests against a government of injustice and coercion? Is it strange that after seeing for centuries such power of oppression wielded by a foreign government the Irish people should believe in a home government?

Their claim for Home Rule for Ireland is justified: —

Because the right of self-government inheres in individuals and in states.

Because it is a crime against the spirit of liberty to govern a state by mere force of numbers and military power, when that state has demanded self-government.

Because the crime is increased when this coercive government is imposed upon a once free people, with race peculiarities and national aspirations.

Because insult is added to injury when such usurpation and coercion are continued under the mockery of constitutional forms.

Home Rule.

Various notions obtain among the Irish themselves, as to wherein Home Rule would affect their present condition. The hillside tenant on the sterile holding where his fathers lived and died, remembers the legends of his childhood, of the wild life of his clan, unfettered by Parliamentary decree or landlord's claim; his dream of Home Rule may be of a life as untrammeled by governmental interference. Others under the sting of oppressive landlordism, and knowing England as the power which sent the armed constable and mounted hussar to enforce the landlord's cruel eviction process, hate England, and believe that a complete separation from her would bring Ireland's national millennium.

But by far the larger and more influential part of the people are intelligent students of political systems; they know the forms of Home Rule under which Canada, Australia and other English colonies maintain harmonious relations with the mother country. They have close connections with the Irish in America and an intimate knowledge of our republican institutions; their leaders in the House of Commons are the peers of English and American statesmen; they desire local government and an Irish Parliament for purely local and Irish affairs, with relations to the Imperial Parliament similar in outline to such as exist between our States and the Government at Washington. They know that the details of these relation will be settled by the power which confers on them local government. They also know that some adjustment of the land question must precede or accompany their desired Home Rule. Mr. Gladstone's measure recognized this necessity, and presented a plan for land purchase.

Knowing the dual nature of the remedy which must be administered to Ireland's diseased body, we remember that during the present century the Imperial Parliament has been again and again informed by its own committees and commissioners, that the land trouble was a comprehensive cause of continued distress. Not until recent years, however, has it attempted to remedy the cause of this distress, but it has by direct legislation augmented the power of the land-

Home Rule. 139

lord and rejected measures offered to alleviate the condition of the tenant.

If Ireland were governed by a Dublin Parliament actually representing the Irish people, such unequal legislation would be unknown. Home Rule would not build better houses for the tenant; it would not mend his fences, reclaim his waste lands 'or teach him better methods of farming; it would not revoice silent mills, restore dismantled factories, reanimate prostrate industries, but with the conscious dignity of self government would come to the people as a whole a responsible activity and the material and social blessings which follow in its train.

Neither can the claim be sustained that the Irish are a vicious people, full of sedition and crime, and thus incapable of self-government. It is reported through authoritative channels that there is less crime in Ireland than in England. The outrages so loudly heralded are features of the agrarian strife which rages and has raged for centuries. This war cannot cease until the free untrammeled cultivation of the soil, and the enjoyment of the results of that labor, are guaranteed to the toiler and actual occupant. It is a matter of surprise that so much oppression has been so patiently endured. The power to bear thus exhibited is an essential element in national independence. An official report given in 1849 by one Captain Kennedy is filled with shocking details of forcible ejectments, some of which had not even the apology of technical legality. The report states, "These ruthless acts of barbarity are submitted to with an unresisting patience hardly credible." To this Sir Robert Peel remarks, "Such tragical instances I do not believe were ever presented, either in point of fact or as conjured up even in the imagination of any human being."

Is not intemperance a fruitful source of poverty and ignorance? Certainly. Ireland is no exception to the rule; drink debases there as it does in England and the United States, although not to any greater extent. The name of Father Mathew is still revered, and his memory yet wields a mighty influence for good. There exists a growing

Home Rule. 141

temperance sentiment, and the League of the Cross is an effective total abstinence society.

Many of the Irish leaders are temperance men, and will be willing and anxious to embody the sentiment of the people in temperance legislation. As stated before, the Irish Parliament years ago desired restrictive legislation, but England refused to listen to the plea, claiming that she must have the revenue!

It is urged by opponents of the Irish cause that Home Rule would be " Rome Rule," and attention is called to the fact that Papacy to-day exerts more complete sway in Ireland than in any country on the earth.

Great apprehension is expressed lest the existing overwhelming Catholic majority in social intercourse, in educational work, in business and trade would grow unbearably arrogant and insufferably intolerant if its present power were supplemented by political ascendency. It is even honestly feared that this ascendency might assume the form of religious persecution, and the future equal the past in secret, if not in open outrage. The history of Ireland proves too much to justify this apprehension. The most appalling outrages of the past have been between opposing faiths, but not chiefly because of these faiths. Hereditary family or tribal feuds, conflicting systems of laws, agrarian controversies, and contested military supremacy, have entailed these inhumanities.

Banners bearing emblems of political faith have been waved, shibboleths of creeds have been uttered, but the real cause has been found in conditions quite foreign to religion or creed.

It was not Puritanism and psalm-singing as opposed to the mass and the confessional that brought gory ascendency to the Cromwellian conquest, neither was inquisitorial malignity the great conspirator in the massacres of 1641 or the rebellion of 1798.

Let it not be forgotten that England was a Catholic country during the earlier centuries of her conquests in Ireland, and that the fruitage of present hatred ripened on trees planted when these nations were of common faith. The parties to the present

Home Rule. 143

controversies are of both faiths; Gladstone is a champion of English Protestantism as represented by the established church, Parnell is a Protestant Dissenter, Dillon and William O'Brien are Catholics, the magistrates before whom O'Brien was tried were also Catholics, as are some of the most obnoxious landlords. Ireland's long controversy has been a revolt against England's policy of conquest, rather than a revolt aginst Protestantism, and Ireland has welcomed the supremacy of Rome as a shield to her civil liberties as well as a dictator of her faith.

At a great meeting in Dublin in the summer of 1887, the presiding officer was the Very Reverend Dr. Walch, archbishop of Dublin, supported on either side by three Protestant members of the House of Commons, who clearly stated their religious faith and boldly declared their willingness to " close up " when the ranks of Ireland's defenders should be thinned by the political, judicial or sanguinary slaughter of their Catholic confrères. No sentiment finds more enthusiastic response than declarations of common interests among those of opposing religious faiths. Is not the love for liberty which finds utterance in the demand for self-government a universal sentiment? Does it not rise to the dignity of a human instinct, always operative, except under individual and national demoralization consequent upon servitude? Will English Protestantism concede that Irish Catholicism is more potent for evil than this universal love of liberty is potent for good? In shame and sorrow do all Protestants remember that the required payments of church tithes from Catholics to the English Protestant Church, and the political disabilities imposed by the English Church and the property disabilities imposed by the English Government upon Irish Catholics are the ghosts of the past that will not down, and before which trembles the Britain of to-day.

The iniquities of the fathers are visited upon the children unto the third and fourth generation, and conscience makes a mighty nation a coward. But bigotry and revenge which may survive tyranny and war, cannot

Home Rule. 145

long exist under the toleration and peace of
political and civil liberty.

To take a retrospective view of the political relations existing between England and Ireland, covering a period of several centuries, to note the conflicting interests there delineated, and to condense these experiences and conflicts into the short space of a few pages, and therefrom render an indictment against any of the later English Parliaments as represented by the Government party then in power, would seem to be an unjust conclusion of the matter.

But when we see by a careful reading of such historical data as have been preserved from destruction, that the Government party in the British Parliament for centuries has almost invariably proceeded in one direction they have seemed to consider the Irish as a distinct race, and not naturally entitled to equal political rights with their own subjects, but that they were natural serfs, ignorant, belligerent and contumacious, having no rights that Englismen were bound to respect, we see how far the habit of power, the greed of wealth, and a worldly vanity upheld by an assumption of religious supremacy, have been efficient in destroying the first simple and pure ideas of righteousness, moral, social and political.

This high and holy principle has been sacrificed times without number.

From such a view we are led to conclude that the indictment against the whole English Government is correct, when this indictment declares that there is scarce one redeeming quality in the policy that has been maintained by that Government during these long years, but rather that there is but little parallel in history, either among barbaric or half-civilized tribes of men, to such rapacious cruelty, such unjust assignment of political rights, as is here presented.

Such, indeed, seems to be the case, and what the leading Christian nation of the world should have done was not to vie with semi-barbaric tribes in all the riot and glut of power after a conquest, but with this power still remaining in their hands, seek to govern by such politic measures as would have assured the conquered people that their real prosperity, order and just law, were the purpose of the dominating power they should have shown; and then the Act of " Union " would have taken possession of the hearts of the Irish people, and the British Empire stand before the world, what she claims herself to be, the rightful exponent of the bravest and best among nations.

Would that it were so, and then we would not be compelled to search long and unsuccessfully for some redeeming quality, some justifying relation of things to excuse these acts of aggressive power.

While we of America condemn England's tardy justice and her actual criminality towards Ireland, let us remember that we are of the same stock; her ancestors are ours; her history until within a little more than a hundred years is our history. We of this young nation have a clear field, an open arena. We have escaped the duty of solving questions which the accretions of time and the complications of dense populations have left in the path of English progress; more severe tests than any yet endured are before this young republic. Shall the smouldering fires of municipal misrule, of the alcoholic liquor traffic, of anarchy, consume our institutions, or shall our struggle with them purify our national character?

What are the evils, and what the remedies? Upon a conscientious solution is the welfare of our nation dependent. Many of these evils are the direct outcome of real and fancied evils in our system of land tenure, which we have seen to be the fruitful cause of Ireland's distress. The careless thinker may scoff, but it is easier to sneer at the theories of Henry George than to patiently study conditions which, even in a land so favored as is ours, already cause distress and suffering. In the immediate past, our ready answer to all suggestions of agrarian discontent has been to point to our immense West. But what was once known as the Great American Desert, now knocks for admission as a State, while pleasant farms and thriving villages fill the territory beyond, once unknown save to the Indian and trapper. Remembering that the best land is always taken first, and that as the quantity of land remaining decreases, so does the quality of the land depreciate, and that much of what was once our country's patrimony is now held by speculative syndicates, many of them composed of foreign aristocrats, we cannot settle the question by drafts upon resources which no longer exist. Our unemployed can no longer be calmly referred to Western land as the panacea for all their complaints. We have had our Haymarket Square. Let us beware lest that sudden outburst become a flowing lava stream of menace. To England, with her crowded population and small area, these problems have come in all their intensity. Similar questions confront us, although the conditions under which they must be solved are much more favorable.

At our first constitutional centennial we do well to set up our monuments of progress, but we do better to observe the ruins of history. Observing these failures in governmental policy, these inhumanities of aggressive power, these disasters of national arrogance, may we avoid a like calamity.

There is nothing more refreshing to pick up in odd minutes than a bright collection out of the poetry of all time of the brightest on almost no matter what subject, even the weather.

Through the Year with the Poets, edited by Oscar Fay Adams. A volume a month of about 140 pages each, with ample indices. 16mo, cloth, 75 cents each; parti-colored cloth, $1.00.

And dainty book-making has much to do with the pleasure of scrappy reading.

New Every Morning, a year-book for girls, by Annie H. Ryder, is a helpful thought or two, out of current writers mainly, for every day in the year; not religious, but chosen for serious aptitude to the state of things in the world we live in. 196 pages. Square 16mo, cloth. $1.00

Notable Prayers of Christian History. By Hezekiah Butterworth. So far as we know, there is no other book in which are gathered the notable prayers of devout men of all times with their biographical and historical connections. 304 pages. 16mo, cloth, 1.00.

Let not the bookseller venture a word on sc abstruse a subject as Browning.

Christmas Eve and Easter Day, and Other Poems. By Robert Browning. Introduction by W. J. Rolfe. The Theory of Robert Browning concerning Personal Immortality by Heloise Edwina Hersey. With notes. 175 pages. 16mo, cloth, 75 cents.

For Browning Classes and Clubs. The text is in very generous type.

Faith and Action is an F. D. Maurice Anthology. Preface by Phillips Brooks. The subjects are: Life, Men, Reforms, Books, Art, Duty, Aspiration, Faith. 269 pages. 12mo, cloth, $1.00.

Quite a new sort of history. School days over, four girl friends return to their homes and life begins. As often happens, life is not as they picture it. What it was for the four and how they met it you shall read in the quiet book.

After School Days. By Christina Goodwin. 196 pages. 12mo, cloth, $1.00.

It is a comforting fact a thousand times that nobody knows, to be sure of it, what is good for him or her. Disappointments are often shorn of their bitterness by the remembrance of it. Often what we look forward to, hope for, strive for, make ourselves anxious about, turns out to be of no particular value; and what we fear and strive against turns out good fortune. Rarely is this practical wisdom made so sure as in this wholesome history out of the stuff that dreams are made of.

A practical help for a girl to surround herself with pleasant things without much shopping. The book is mainly filled with ways to exercise taste on waste or picked-up things for use with an eye to decoration as well.

For a Girl's Room. By Some Friends of the Girls. 236 pages. 12mo, cloth, $1.00.

A friendly sort of a book to fill odd minutes, whether at home or out, for herself or another. By no means on "fancy-work"—not all work— Chapter XXI is How to Tame Birds and XXV is What to Do in Emergencies.

How to Cook Well is promising title. The author, J. Rosalie Benton. We light on this sentence on breakfast: "Yet in how many families is it the custom to send the master of the house to his daily round of business with an unsatisfied feeling after partaking of a hurried meal altogether unpalatable!" That is still more promising. There are 400 pages of performance. 12mo, cloth, $1.50.

One of the ways to get some notions of things into young folks' heads without any work on their part is to tell them stories and weave in the knowledge.

Another way is to make a book of such stories. The book has the advantage of the story-teller. It can be full of pictures; and one can be more careful in making a book than in talking. If his memory slips a little, he can stop and hunt up the facts.

Story Book of Science. By Lydia Hoyt Farmer. Illustrated. 330 pages. 12mo, cloth, $1.50.

There are twenty different stories and seventy five pictures. A surprising number of bits of knowledge are woven and pictured in; and the book is as light and easy as if it were nonsense.

There's so much to know nowadays. Children have to begin before they know it.

Waifs and their Authors is a collection, by A. A. Hopkins, of poetry worthy of preservation, mainly out of newspapers and by living writers not yet ranked as Poets — with notes, personal, biographical, critical, genial always, under twenty-one names. 317 pages.

The Family Flights, by Edward Everett Hale and Susan Hale, are a series of book journeys through the several countries with eyes and ears wide open, old eyes and young eyes, and ears. The books are full of pictures, and fuller of knowledge not only of what is going on but what has gone on ever since book-making began, and fuller yet of brightness and interest. You see the old as old; but you see it; you see where it was and the marks it left. You see the new with eyes made sharper by knowledge of what has gone on in the world.

In other words these books amount to something like going through these places with a traveling-companion who knows all about them and their histories.

They are written and pictured for boys and girls: but there is nothing to hinder the old folks going along. Will you go?

Family Flight through France, Germany, Norway and Switzerland. 405 pages.
Family Flight over Egypt and Syria. 388 pages.
Family Flight through Spain. 360 pages.
Family Flight around Home (which means about Boston) 366 pages.
Family Flight through Mexico. 300 pages.
Each 8vo, boards, $1.75 ; cloth, $2.25.

One of the most effective means of exciting and satisfying zeal for knowledge of the world we have in books.

A good book for young folks is Ned Melbourne's Mission, not too good to have a spice of life and adventure, but with that indirect influence for good thinking and good doing that is more potent than a sermon to young people.

Ned Melbourne's Mission. 12mo, cloth, $1.50.

www.ingramcontent.com/pod-product-compliance
Lightning Source LLC
Chambersburg PA
CBHW030312170426
43202CB00009B/980